CH00937662

Born in Leeds the James 'Jock' Wilkinson spent four and a half years living in Bangalore. This book is about that time. On return from India he joined the R.A.F and trained as a fast jet pilot. A medical condition terminated this career. Following graduation from Leeds university the James spent thirty years teaching. Completing an M.A, he retired, and now spends his time fly-fishing, painting portraits, play classical guitar and acrylic landscapes.

Dedicated to my wife, Carol, who had no idea what her crazy husband had gotten up to in his youth until she read this book.

James 'Jock' Wilkinson

SHIKARI SHAITAN

AUSTIN MACAULEY PUBLISHERS™

LONDON • CAMBRIDGE • NEW YORK • SHARJAH

Copyright © James 'Jock' Wilkinson 2022

The right of James 'Jock' Wilkinson to be identified as author of this work has been asserted by the author in accordance with sections 77 and 78 of the Copyright, Designs and Patents Act 1988.

All rights reserved. No part of this publication may be reproduced, stored in a retrieval system, or transmitted in any form or by any means, electronic, mechanical, photocopying, recording, or otherwise, without the prior permission of the publishers.

Any person who commits any unauthorised act in relation to this publication may be liable to criminal prosecution and civil claims for damages.

All of the events in this memoir are true to the best of author's memory. The views expressed in this memoir are solely those of the author.

A CIP catalogue record for this title is available from the British Library.

ISBN 9781398420830 (Paperback)
ISBN 9781398420847 (Hardback)
ISBN 9781398420854 (ePub e-book)

www.austinmacauley.com

First Published 2022
Austin Macauley Publishers Ltd®
1 Canada Square
Canary Wharf
London
E14 5AA

Table of Contents

Hunting the Devil

or

The Misadventures of an Englishman in India

The Prologue

I arrived in India, as a nineteen-year-old, just fourteen days after my birthday. The company that I worked for had decided to use a consistent office system throughout its business empire around the world, so having volunteered to teach our system to our overseas offices, I found myself heading for Bangalore in southern India. Thus began a series of misadventures that I have recounted in the following pages. I soon found out that not only did I do very little tutoring, but rather, I found myself employed on an unpaid and unofficial basis as a pest controller by various government offices and departments, as they discovered that I had absolutely no imagination about the consequences of picking an argument with large anti-social members of the cat family and coupled that with a complete faith in my own ability to use firearms. I might add that at this time, organisations such as Operation Tiger did not exist.

I have used firearms of various types since I was eleven years old, so it will come as no surprise for you to find that I took to hunting in India, like the proverbial duck to water. Coupled with the fact that various villagers back in England, as well as my own grandfather, a retired coal miner, taught me more about poaching and tracking and the ways of wildlife than any upright and law-abiding citizen has any right to know.

It is hardly surprising that I took great pleasure in hunting the forests of southern India.

At the time I am writing about, there was no government organised system for dealing with maneaters or rogues. Such problems were left to the amateur hunter, and whilst many hunters shot tigers and panthers, very few considered hunting maneaters. It was a form of hunting that was considered to be too risky and too dangerous! Afterall, these animals kill people.

There are, no doubt, people who will decry the hunting of any of the big cats. To those people, I offer my apologies for offending their sensibilities, particularly today when many species are verging on extinction, but when you have seen the fear and trepidation caused by these homicidal felines, then I think you must accept the necessity of what I did. Read the account of the *Killer from Kouthalu* to get some idea of fear and terror. Also, would we allow a murderer, such as the Yorkshire Ripper, to continue unchecked? Surely, the answer is no. Therefore, you cannot allow a killer cat to continue its career. It needs to be stopped, and I spent nearly five years of my life trying to stop them. Let me make a confession, right now. I absolutely adore the big cats and I would be deliriously happy if no more were killed. Instead, I would like to see them returned to their former numbers. Sadly, this will not happen, because wildlife is in competition with the human race and there can be only one winner!

Aside from my hunting activities, my sojourn in India allowed me to meet some amazing characters, none more so than my personal servant or bearer, a gentleman from the top of his turban to the toes of his immaculately polished riding boots, a Sikh by the name of Govind Singh Negri. He taught

11

me more about dealing with people and general growing up than I could ever have imagined possible. Thank you, my friend! Also, worthy of mention is Roga, a Chenchu, who taught me about tracking the big cats and the ways of the jungle and the man who introduced me to Roga, my friend David Kerr, mentor, font of wisdom, and probably the reason I survived to write this book. Thank you.

Why do carnivores turn to man eating? According to the late, great Colonel Jim Corbett, only about one in a thousand big cats turn to a diet of human flesh. Why do they do this? According to Corbett, approximately ten percent of maneaters resort to the change of diet because they can no longer hunt their normal prey due to old age, such as the Maneater of the Babur Badans. The remaining ninety percent make the change because of injury or the effects of shooting, leaving the cat wounded and unable to pursue its normal prey, such as the Pulivalam Maneater. Also, we must accept that the big cats do not know that the human race is a protected species and off limits and that humans take a very dim view of murder, no matter who or what commits the murderous deed. The carnivores are, simply, pursuing a hairless monkey that is relatively easy to catch and kill and will feed them for five or six days. No wonder, that in exceptional circumstances, the carnivores take to man eating!

There are exceptions to any rule and the Magadi maneater was one such exception, in that there was no discernible reason for the tigress to take up the pernicious practice of man eating. But she did! To read some accounts that have been written about the Indian jungle, you could be forgiven for thinking that if you journey into the jungles, your chances of survival are slight. There could be nothing further from the truth. Left to their own devices, the average big cat will avoid any form of confrontation. I spent many nights in the jungles of southern India with no firearms and my only security and warmth being a small fire. At no time did I feel threatened. Some situations need care. Lone elephants or an area where a declared maneater is operating are to be avoided. Yet millions of Indians work in the forests, every day, without suffering any harm and they must, by all the laws of averages, have walked past wild animals of all kinds without knowing that the animal was there.

Chapter 1
The Shirlal Maneater

Shirlal is a tiny hamlet of about eight or nine mud and thatch huts within the Shirlal forest range, in the foothills of the Nilgiri Hills. Shirlal, itself, is almost due west of the city of Bangalore. Once the traveller turns off the main road, a cart track is followed through thick vegetation to within about a mile of the village, the rest of the route being covered on foot, as the track becomes impassable to any form of motorised vehicle, including my WWII Jeep! Shirlal is one of a group of small villages or hamlets within the bounds of the Shirlal forest block.

Peace and tranquillity seemed to ooze from the very fabric of the hamlet, and had done for many years, but this illusion of the idyllic was about to be shattered. Occasionally, a dog or goat would disappear from Shirlal or one of its nearby neighbouring villages. As is often the case in India, nobody took any notice of these events, ascribing the disappearances to unlucky circumstances, or the will of the Gods.

The 'Greybeards' among the villagers, however, expressed the view that in years gone by, similar events had presaged the manifestation of a maneater. They warned anyone who would listen, about the possible consequences, but as is often the case, the young thought they knew better than their elders. Most of the villagers ignored the words of warning and dismissed them as the senile ramblings of the elderly.

Nathu, a woodcutter, was making his way home late in the evening. Shadows cast by the setting sun made the task of the silent watcher far easier as it noted with satisfaction that Nathu was alone. Every few yards along his walk, Nathu would stop and listen for the ominous rumble of a large stomach or the breaking of branches that would indicate the presence of a feeding elephant. Lone elephants are to be avoided at all costs, as I will explain later, in chapter eight. Dusk was settling in, and in less than half an hour, it would be night and visibility would be greatly impaired. Nathu was about a quarter of a mile from Shirlal and in his hurry to arrive home, before dark, he increased his pace. But he failed to register the fact that the jungle had fallen silent. No birds twittered, even the Langur monkeys had fallen silent. To anyone in the know and being observant this silence would have carried one message: 'Beware, a large carnivore is nearby'. However, even if he had not moved faster, it is very doubtful that Nathu would have heard anything or noticed the malevolent, unflinching, yellow eyes of the Thendu or large forest dwelling panther, that followed his every move.

The panther waited for its opportunity. The muscles along its flank trembled as it poised itself for the charge that would surely come. Nathu was about one hundred yards from the village when the attack was launched. The panther may have issued the grunting roar that panthers make when they charge, Nathu may have heard the soft fall of the panther's pads on the forest path – it is, perhaps, better to assume that Nathu saw and heard nothing! The panther hit Nathu in the middle of the back. He managed to scream once before the four large fangs met in his neck, breaking his spine and causing instantaneous death as he hit the dirt track under the weight of a hundred and sixty pounds of bone and muscle.

In the village, several villagers heard the single scream, but fearing the noise to be the work of forest demons, nobody was prepared to sally forth to find the source of the noise, or to render assistance to the maker of the scream! Even if they had done so, Nathu was beyond help.

The following morning, well after sunrise, a group of about twelve people, that included Nathu's wife, set forth to find him. They had travelled about a hundred yards when one of their number noticed rust-coloured splashes in the dirt of the path – blood! Signs of a large object being dragged were visible in the long grass. Slowly and carefully, in great trepidation and fear, the party followed the drag for about thirty yards until they found all that was left of the late Nathu, under a large thorn bush. The panther had eaten the chest, buttocks and shoulders of the cadaver, leaving the head, arms, and legs. These remaining bits were hastily gathered together and taken back to the village for cremation.

Nathu's death might have been recorded as an unfortunate accident, but a week later, a pregnant bride of some fifteen summers was taken as she visited a stream to collect water. Her body was never found, but the signs and pug marks by the stream told the story most clearly. She had been taken by a large male panther, somewhat past his prime. An animal that was lame in its off-front leg, as could be seen by the impression of a stump rather than the customary pug marks. Fear hung over the village and at night, every hut was barred and barricaded better than Fort Knox.

Over the next thirty months, the panther accounted for a total of twenty-eight victims. This showed quite clearly that the cat was surviving on game as well as humans, as a killing every month would not sustain the panther. At this point, Indian bureaucracy, never renowned for the alacrity of its decision making, decided that enough was enough. As a result, it published the usual notice in the Forestry Department gazette, advertising the fact that the Shirlal block was now open to all license holders who may wish to shoot the recalcitrant panther. However, as Shirlal was in a remoter part of the Nilgiris in the Western Ghats, nobody seemed inclined to spend days or weeks pushing their way through the dense undergrowth looking for the panther, with the very real possibility of having a large and, decidedly, anti-social cat grabbing the hunter by the scruff of the neck. Ouch!

I was sitting in the breakfast room of the bungalow that my employers had kindly provided for me in the village of Whitefields, just a few miles from Bangalore. My bearer, Govind, came in and presented me with the latest copy of the Forestry Gazette. I read through the paper and noted the paragraph about the Shirlal panther. I had lived in India for a few months but, already, the notion of shooting big game had grown to compulsive proportions. During my short sojourn in India, I had become friends with a man called David Kerr, a man who had lived in India all his life and who had an impressive list of maneaters to his credit. I had sought his help and advice on the subject of hunting maneaters. David worked on the principle that the best way to learn about hunting maneaters was by hunting them – a line of reasoning that was difficult to argue with. I decided that as you have to start somewhere, the Shirlal panther would be as good as any to start on. Such is the arrogance of youth – some would say the stupidity of youth.

Losing no time, I sent a telegram to the District Forest Officer (D.F.O.) making two conditions on which I would be prepared to hunt the panther. These conditions were:

1. All monetary rewards would be cancelled – I had no desire to be considered a mercenary.
2. The other hunters – in fact, there were none – would be called on to vacate the block, as I had no desire to be shot by accident, in mistake for a panther. Such mistakes have happened!

A telegram arrived within a day from the D.F.O. agreeing to my request and offering me the cooperation of all members of the Forestry Department and local villagers. There could be no going back; I was committed to the venture.

Govind loaded everything I could possibly need into my Willy's Jeep. I cleaned and checked my rifle – a sporting model Lee-Enfield chambered for the 303 Nitro express, a very effective and accurate cat stopper. I climbed into the Jeep and set off towards Shirlal. Eventually, I reached the point where I could go no further in the jeep on that awful cart track. Leaving the jeep, I shouldered my large rucksack and set off for the village, noting that I had plenty of time to reach Shirlal before darkness fell. I would, perhaps, have had my equilibrium seriously disturbed if I had known that this track was a favourite section for the maneater finding its meals!

Arriving at the village, the most immediate impression was one of abject terror. People poked their heads out of huts but came no further, until they realised that I had arrived to help them. Then, they emerged to tell me all about their trials and tribulations at the fangs of the maneater and beseech me for help! Next impression was the horrific smell of human excrement. Not surprising, as the huts were surrounded by heaps of human waste. People were so frightened that they were not prepared to follow the basic rules of hygiene and walk into the forest to answer the calls of nature. Because of these problems, I decided to pitch my tent a hundred yards or so, from the hamlet. My tent was modelled on the Black's 'Itesa' and provided me with an ideal shelter on my hunting trips. I had the village headman arrange for a thorn barricade to be put up round the tent to make sure I did not have any unwelcome visitors in the night. Whilst I was pitching my tent, the headman told me that the maneater often visited the village during the hours of darkness. This was amply demonstrated by the multiplicity of scratch marks on virtually all the doors in the village.

Having imparted all, they knew about the panther, the villagers hurried off to the barricaded safety of their huts, leaving me to focus my thoughts on the panther. One thing was certain: I would gain nothing except collecting some very nasty scars, at best, if I attempted to go blundering about in dense jungle looking for the panther in the pitch black of the night. I decided that it would be more profitable (and considerably safer) to spend the night sat inside my tent on a small folding camp-chair with my Lee-Enfield across my knees and my torch close at hand. I cleared a small entrance in the thorn fence, directly in front of the tent door, hoping that this would guide the panther directly into my line of fire.

It was a very bright, moon-lit night. Through the doorway of the tent, I could see a myriad of stars in the clear, cloudless sky. Once my eyes had become adjusted to the light, I found I could see remarkably well. Even so, to say that I was tensed up would be an understatement. I could feel the stock of my rifle growing sweaty under my grip, so I quickly wiped my hand on my trousers. Fortunately, my hat had a leather head band that absorbed the moisture from my sweaty brow, so my sight was not impaired by droplets of sweat falling into my eyes. After about two hours, I poured myself a drink of tea from my thermos flask. My frayed nerves had settled down a little by this time. I had just put the cup back on top of the flask when I was convinced, I heard a rustle, albeit very softly, outside the tent. My heart rate shot up and I noticed the distinctly coppery taste of fear in my mouth. I pointed the muzzle of the rifle towards the gap in the fence and pushed the safety-catch into the 'fire' position. Again, I heard the soft noise of something gently dragging in the dirt. I raised the rifle to my shoulder and aimed at the gap.

What came next certainly took me by surprise and was completely unexpected. A timorous voice pleaded from out of the dark. "Don't shoot! Don't shoot!" I shone the torch out of the door in the direction of where I thought the voice had come from. Eventually, my torch beam alighted on the most abject face I have ever seen. The eyes of the individual were dilated like a couple of saucers, sweat was streaming down his face and soaking into his shirt. His teeth were chattering like castanets at a Spanish dance contest. I grabbed him by the shirt and pulled him into the enclosure and then into my tent. I sat him down on my camp bed and asked him, none too politely, if he was aware that a man-eating panther was operating in the area. The man averred that he knew, only too well about the panther. He told me that his name was Kunthi and that he lived in a village about ten miles away. He had been gathering honey, when he noticed that the jungle was turning dark. Knowing about the panther, Kunthi had panicked, and in rushing about in the undergrowth, he had become completely disorientated and lost in the pitch dark of the jungle. Finally, when he was reaching the point of screaming his head off, he had blundered onto my tent and in trying to find his way in, he had made the noise that I had first noticed. He had heard the metallic click of the safety-catch being pushed off and realised that someone with a rifle was in the tent, hence his heartfelt plea for me not to shoot.

Kunthi continued to sit on my camp bed with his teeth chattering. I assumed, wrongly, that this reaction was because of the cold, so I made him lay down and threw my blanket over him. The noise did not stop, even with his head buried in my bedding. How I was supposed to hear the approach of the panther with this sort of distraction, I did not know! Did he think he was the only one who was scared? My stomach had a squadron of butterflies performing formation aerobatics in it and the hairs on the back of my neck were stood on end performing a tango! Finally, in an act of desperation, I asked Kunthi to sit on the edge of the bed and wrapped in the blanket, he was to hold my torch and shine it out of the tent when I gave the instruction. He agreed to my request, and this seemed to take his mind off the panther, because his teeth stopped chattering. We settled down to watch through the long night hours in what was to prove one of the most anxious and stressful periods of time I have ever endured.

At about three-thirty in the morning, I heard a gentle rustle in the surrounding jungle. I nudge Kunthi, but he had also heard the noise. Could this be the panther I asked myself?

With experience, I would have noticed that the Nightjars and Brain Fever birds were still chattering. These birds are very noticeably silent when a big cat is in the vicinity. They are, also, very vociferous in voicing their alarm calls when they spot a big cat. Not knowing this, I prepared for the appearance of the panther. The rustling stopped, almost opposite the entrance to the barricade. I listened for the hissing noise that I had been told that panthers make just prior to a charge, but I could hear nothing. I whispered to Kunthi, "Battery *poddu*. Shine the torch." Kunthi made no move, but his teeth were chattering again. Once more I whispered to him to shine the torch. Again, inactivity was his reaction.

In desperation, I grabbed the torch from his apparently lifeless hand. With difficulty, I held the torch against the fore end of the rifle. Pointed the rifle in the direction of the noise and pressed the 'on' switch, expecting to see the panther. To my surprise, the beam of the torch revealed a porcupine snuffling past the entrance to the enclosure. With this revelation, my heart rate dropped from about a thousand beats a minute to a more manageable five hundred beats a minute. Even the squadron of butterflies seemed to have departed for another aerodrome! The porcupine waddled away, totally oblivious to the damage he had done to my life expectancy!

With the immediate panic over, we settled down to await the dawn. With the manifestation of the true dawn, we emerged from the tent and wandered over to the village. The villagers very kindly offered me and my companion breakfast. I decided that Kunthi would not be safe walking back to his own village alone, so I decided to walk with him. Subsequent events would prove that I do have the occasional moments of lucid thought. We set off at about eight in the morning, following the track through the forest.

We had been walking for about two hours when we approached a gulley between two large piles of rock. For no logical reason, I suddenly developed a very uncomfortable feeling about this obstacle. I could not put a reason to this apprehension, but the feeling would not go away. The hairs on the back of my neck were stood on end and I had feelings of serious apprehension about passing those rocks. Particularly, a large cleft that started at about five feet above the ground and was wide enough to accommodate a panther, attracted my attention. The jungle was too dense to allow a detour, so we would have to face the track through the rocks.

I told Kunthi to walk in front of me and that if he saw or heard the panther, he was to throw himself on the path, quickly, to give me shooting room. I noticed that a gentle breeze was blowing from my right, so the attack, if it came, would be from my left, and being the last man in the line, I was very likely to be the target of the panther's attack. Very slowly, we edged forward. I had my rifle to my shoulder and my finger was down the outside of the trigger guard.

As we drew level with the cleft I stared hard into the darkness of the cleft and thought I saw a slightly darker shadow back in the recess. The shadow seemed to move in a blur of darkness and at the same time a low growl came from the darkness. I grabbed hold of Kunthi, then pointed towards a few stones by the side of the track. I, then, pointed towards the cleft. Kunthi got the idea. He threw a stone into the cleft, then nimbly stepped aside, to leave me with rifle to shoulder waiting for the charge that I was convinced would be launched. The charge never came. The maneater had decided that the cleft was not a healthy place to be! Experience would teach me that such a course of action was not uncommon as maneaters seem to have a well-developed sense of self-preservation that seems to warn them that some humans (particularly those carrying firearms) are potentially hazardous to their health.

An hour later, we arrived at Kunthi's village, where his friends and family made it clear they were very glad to see him alive. After a mug of tea, I started back towards Shirlal. I had been walking for an hour, taking care to avoid bushes and shadows that might conceal the maneater. Just before I reached the pile of rocks with the cleft, I heard voices calling, "*Sahib, sahib!*" I halted and called back to the men who, within a few minutes, had found me. They had come from a nearby village and informed me that a goatherd had not returned the previous evening, but they had gone out to look for him early in the morning. They had found him, or rather they had found what was left of him, underneath a Ficus tree.

The villagers took me towards the scene of the tragedy. I could hear the flies long before I could see the cadaver. The body was completely covered from one end to the other by the writhing blue mass of flies. Judging by the reaction of the villagers, in that they hurriedly covered their noses and mouths, the corpse must have been very smelly. Fortunately, my nose had been cauterised up both nostrils about a year earlier and, so, I had absolutely no sense of smell. Plans were soon made. A small *machan* (a tree platform for shooting dangerous game) was constructed about fifteen feet from the ground. When the *machan* was completed, I shinned up the tree and pulled my rifle after me. Fortunately, I had my water bottle and my pipe for company. The men left, and keeping close together, headed back to their village.

I am, fortunately, one of those people who are quite happy with their own company, so I spent my time watching the activities in the jungle, noting with some satisfaction that the birds and the Langur monkeys had not registered my presence. The heat was unpleasant and oppressive, but I consoled myself with the knowledge that as night came on, it would grow very chilly. In India, it goes from complete daylight to inky darkness in about fifteen minutes, and today was no exception. Night clamped in and visibility was only a few yards until the moon and stars emerged from behind the clouds. Then, I could see for about twenty-five yards. Not expecting to have this opportunity to shoot the maneater, I had not brought a torch, so I would have to rely on my night vision if I got a chance of a shot.

About three hours had passed since night fall. I looked at the luminous face of my watch. As I did so, I heard a slight hissing sound coming from the direction of a group of bushes about twenty yards away. I knew what the sound was, it was a panther expelling air through its teeth. It is the sound the cat makes when trying to decide whether or not to charge. The panther must have become aware of my presence, but the question that taxed me was 'how?' I had made no sound. I had sat cross-legged, without moving, since I had climbed into the *machan* about seven hours ago. Then the realisation struck me that the panther must have been aware of my presence from the outset and the only way it could have done that was by actually watching me climb the tree. This meant that the panther must have been very close to the kill when the men were building the *machan* – I reckon that somebody in that group of men had been very lucky not to have a large, angry panther wrapped around their throat! The question, now, arose of 'what happens next?' That question was soon answered. The panther began to circle the tree I was perched in and at the same time, growling loudly. The cat took great care not to be seen and continued to growl and circle the area. It continued in this fashion for the next two or three hours. I was feeling totally comfortable about the situation because, if I could hear the panther, I knew exactly where it was and what it was doing. It was the occasional silences that caused me worry, as I had to rely on my hearing to identify any sounds that could indicate the panther was creeping towards me or, even worse, was trying to climb the tree I was perched in.

Eventually dawn broke and as it did so, a group of men arrived from the village. The panther had departed when it heard the men approach. Their attendance was twofold in intent. Firstly, they wanted to find out if I had been fortunate in my vigil and had shot the panther when it returned to its kill. The second reason was to remove the body and take it for cremation. This course of action left me without a reason for the panther to return but was a perfectly understandable reaction by the distraught relatives.

I left the villagers and set off on my return journey to Shirlal. There, the villagers wanted to know what had happened and why? I related my adventures and then disappeared into my tent to make up for my lost slumbers. When I woke, I focussed my mind on what to do next. It seemed to me that to blunder around in the surrounding jungle looking for the cat did not offer much chance of success. My best hope seemed to be to wait for the panther in an area that it visited on a frequent basis and that meant in a village. One of the huts in the village was vacant. So, it was agreed that I would sit in the hut, as far back from the doorway as possible, and await the turn of events. I fastened my torch to the stock of the rifle and taking a blanket to keep warm, together with a flask of tea and my pipe, settled down to my night vigil. Smoking my pipe helped me to keep awake and because I was supposed to be a villager spending a night in the hut, the act of smoking should not alarm the panther. The night proved to be a long and dreary watch, and in a fit of disgust, I returned to my tent and fell asleep whilst casting grave doubts on the panther's parentage and ancestry! I continued to follow this course of action for the next three nights. I had just entered the hut for the third night, when a group of men approached the hut. It was late afternoon, and the sun was about half an hour from setting. The men informed me that a forester had been chopping trees when he had been taken by the panther. This event had happened about a mile from Shirlal, about an hour earlier. The men assured me that if I hurried, I would be able to catch the panther on its kill.

As this information was being imparted to me, I was struck by the artless way that villagers throughout India expect you to risk your beautiful, young body without the villagers giving the slightest thought for your wellbeing! I was not over keen to hunt the panther on foot in a dense jungle, at night, for very obvious reasons. However, this was my best opportunity, without a doubt, to deal with the panther. Therefore, regardless of my apprehension, the opportunity would have to be seized to shoot the cat. My informants told me that the best way to find the kill would be to walk due west from the village, until I met a dry nullah or riverbed that ran at right angles to my original direction of travel. After entering the nullah, I was to turn to my right and proceed for about four-hundred yards until the nullah almost doubled back on itself. At this point, I was to leave the nullah and proceed at a declination of about 45 degrees to my original track. The panther and/or body would be found in about 400 yards, hence.

I checked my rifle and torch to make sure that they were both working and set off on my lonely walk. It was now becoming dark, and visibility was not good. I was very concerned that I might step on a snake, in the dark. The Puff Adder, in particular, was a nasty customer with rotatable fangs about an inch in length. The poison would take about twelve hours to kill the victim, but I had no desire to test the voracity of the herpetologist's pronunciations on the toxicity of the venom. This snake tends to lay on forest paths, at night, absorbing the heat from the ground. My thick leather jungle boots should provide some protection if I trod on one in the dark, but I would not like to rely on that act of good fortune. The soft, crepe soles of my jungle boots would provide no warning for the snake to get out of my way until it was too late!

Slowly and carefully, I walked along the path until I reached the nullah. I stopped and listened for a few minutes, but I could hear nothing. Carefully, I slipped over the edge of the nullah and then stood on its bed, which was about four feet lower than the surrounding land. The moon and stars had started to illuminate the ground so that I could see for about thirty yards. Since the age of eleven, I had been accustomed to walking the fields and woods of my native Yorkshire in the dark, so the darkness held no fears for me, but the fact that I was pursuing a large and very anti-social panther certainly grabbed my attention! Fear is a wonderful focus of attention. In consequence, I proceeded very carefully, taking great care to ensure that I did not tread on a leaf or kick a stone, or brush against any shrubbery on my passage down the nullah. I don't know how long it took to reach the bend I had been told about, as looking at your watch is pointless and an unnecessary as well as a dangerous distraction. When I reached the bend I stopped, rested my rifle on the top of the bank, folded my arms and rested on the top of the bank. I listened carefully for about five minutes, but I heard nothing except the calling of birds of the night such as the nightjar, the 'Did you, do it?' Bird, or the night heron. Without making a sound, I inched myself out of the nullah, got to my feet and set off in the direction I had been given. The jungle was very dense, and to avoid making any noise, I had to walk around bushes instead of through them.

After I had walked for about four hundred yards, I stopped to listen. At first, I heard nothing. The silence was deafening! Then after a few minutes, I heard the unmistakable sound of bones being crunched. The panther was on its kill and was busy feeding. My problem was that the sound was coming from some distance to my left. I had walked too far to my right, in my efforts to avoid forcing my way through the undergrowth, and, thereby, making a noise that would advertise my presence to the panther. It should be noted that the big cats can hear a wristwatch at fifty yards! So, the need to be very quiet and circumspect was of the utmost importance, especially with respect to my health and well-being. I set off very slowly towards the sound, knowing that for as long as I could hear the panther, I was safe from attack. I inched my way forward, listening to the growing sounds of the panther

29

feeding. Suddenly, the sounds ceased! To say that the sound of silence was frightening would be an understatement of monumental proportions. The butterflies were back and performing formation aerobatics, again! I listened, intently, but could hear nothing. Then I heard the sibilant hiss that a panther makes just before launching an attack. I flicked the torch on and raised the rifle to my shoulder, at the same time flicking the safety catch to the fire position. About thirty yards away, the torch illuminated the crouching shape of the panther. I was actually squeezing the trigger, as the panther threw itself sideways and disappeared into the scrub, with a low growl. Once again, the sense of self-preservation that all maneaters seem to possess had warned the panther that it was being lined-up for a prefrontal lobotomy. It decided not to hang around.

I was now in a panic! Where was the panther and, most importantly, what were its intentions towards me? Then my brain took over and I asked myself the sensible question of where was the breeze blowing from? Because the panther would – following the laws of nature – stalk me into wind and would launch an attack from the same direction. In fact, I could feel the breeze on the back of my neck, so any attack would come from the opposite direction or from the side. I noted that a small tree stood about ten yards from the body. Around the trunk, for a radius of about five yards, was scattered a thick blanket of dried leaves. If anything trod on those leaves, I would get a clear warning of any approach. I walked over to the tree and sat down with my back to the trunk and the wind blowing from behind the tree. I don't know how much pipe tobacco was consumed by my vigil, but it had the desired effect of keeping me awake. At about three in the morning, a hyena approached the body and as it bent down to sniff at the corpse, I told it in Hindi to go away! The hyena uttered a 'chee, chee, chee' of alarm and disappeared into the night at a fair old speed. It, apparently, did not like dead bodies that spoke to it in Hindi. Things settled down, and I continued my watch.

Dawn broke and I stood up and stretched my legs. The birds of the jungle and the behaviour of the Langur monkeys told me that the panther was not in the immediate vicinity. The sun had been up about an hour, when a group of villagers approached. They had come to collect the cadaver for cremation. Together, we returned to Shirlal. I had, now, been hunting our homicidal cat for nearly three weeks and seemed to be getting no closer to achieving my goal.

I returned to my tent, pulled the thorn barrier into place and slept for about five hours. I got up and sat on my camp chair, drinking tea and smoking my pipe. I thought about the situation and decided that unless there was a body over which I could sit, my best option was to sit in the hut and await a visitation from the panther. Accordingly, late in the afternoon, I entered the hut I had used previously and made myself as comfortable as possible.

As night fell, my eyes became accustomed to the darkness and the combination of moon and stars, together with a cloudless sky that enabled me to see the huts opposite. I sat on my camp chair, listening to the inhabitants of the huts chattering away. Slowly, the voices died away, and apart from the odd bout of snoring, everything became quiet. About two in the morning, a dog barked from within one of the huts, to be followed by a couple of additional dogs giving tongue. This meant that at least one of the dogs had scented the panther; this meant the cat was in the village and on the prowl! After a while, I thought I heard a noise at the back of the hut, then, there came the confirmation, as I heard the cat scratching at the wall of the hut behind my back. I pushed the safety catch on the Lee-Enfield to the fire position and, at the same time, rested my thumb on the switch of the torch fastened underneath the barrel. The next fifteen minutes passed in an eternity of time. What would happen next?

I had not taken my eyes off the area of village revealed by the open door, when I became conscious of a shape against the hut opposite me, that had not been there a minute earlier. I pressed the button on the torch and the beam illuminated the crouching form of a panther. The panther whirled around preparatory to making a bolt for the surrounding jungle. I noted that the sights were aligned just behind the panther's right shoulder. I squeezed the trigger, and in response to the sound of the shot, the cat leapt in the air, let out a shriek and disappeared into the jungle. My worst fears had been realised! I had only wounded the cat and could, now, look forward to being stalked by a panther, hell-bent on revenge. I had heard stories of such events and they did not inspire me with confidence. I had no wish to finish the night looking like a bowl of cat food. Hands up those who would like to have their body radically rearranged by a very angry cat. I sat, unmoving, watching the doorway and as much of the village as was possible, trying to make sure I did not get surprised by 160 pounds of homicidal intent. Voices called from the huts asking me if I had shot the cat. At the top of my voice, I replied that the cat was in the hamlet and that everyone would be best served by keeping very quiet. The silence in that hamlet was amazing. Not a sound could be heard. Dawn broke and I emerged from the hut, having suffered the anxiety of the inexperienced, since firing at the cat.

Accompanied by most of the hamlet, I walked over to the point where I believed the cat had been standing when I fired the shot. On the ground was a streak of thick blood. So, I had hit the panther. The next question was where had the cat gone and what was I going to do about the situation. I would have to follow the blood trail into the thick jungle. Everyone who had offered me advice on hunting the big cats had stressed that panthers are very astute, and diabolically cunning when wounded. They do not favour the frontal charge, instead they prefer the freebie from the rear or the side. There were stories of wounded cats being peppered with buckshot, or having large stones bounced off them, without once betraying their presence. Instead, they will hide behind any available cover until they are convinced that they cannot miss you, then they will launch their attack and nine times out of ten, this would be from the rear and at very close range. This could be very interesting!

I fastened a pullover around my neck, on the principle that in the event of an attack from the rear, the panther just might get tangled in the wool, giving me a chance to shove the muzzle of the rifle into its mouth and stamp it as cancelled. At least, that was the theory. Isn't theory a wonderful thing? I set off, following the dried blood trail. I was moving very slowly and walking on the outsides of my boots to reduce any possible sounds that I might make to a minimum. I was holding the rifle well back on my hip to make sure that the panther could not come between the muzzle of the rifle and me. It took me about thirty minutes to cover the forty yards I had travelled when I became convinced that I could see the profile of the panther, in a clump of particularly thick undergrowth. Only the front of the head was visible, camouflaged as it was by the rosettes on its head and the dappled sunshine on the foliage. I lined the sights of the Lee-Enfield on where I thought its left ear was and squeezed the trigger. The cat fell towards me, without making a sound or any movement. I looked around and found a large stone. I picked it up and threw it with my left hand. It bounced off the body of the cat, with no response. Slowly, I walked over to the panther and confirmed that the panther was dead, cold, and stiff! I called to the waiting villagers and assured them that the panther was dead. The villagers arrived in minutes, and they came crowding around to see their dead enemy. The body was carried to my camp and my tent, then everything was packed away and carried to my jeep. I wished my newfound friends goodbye and drove to the Forestry Office and left the panther as proof I had shot the maneater. Everyone noted that it had a right front pad that left no pug mark as such. I had obviously shot the correct animal. The D.F.O. was delighted. I drove home to Bangalore.

After I had unpacked, I called to see my mentor, David Kerr. Talking to him, I learnt some very important lessons. Firstly, when a big cat jumps the way that the panther did, it meant it had been shot through the heart and, in effect, was dead. Secondly, the amount and thickness of the blood meant an arterial wound, and this would produce death very quickly. Finally, you must take your time when tracking and do not rush. I had survived my first hunt and had learnt a great deal. Not least was how to survive!

The Shirlal maneater had killed a total of thirty people. It's hunting days were well and truly over and the people of

Shirlal could live in peace and free from fear. Finally, on skinning the animal, it became apparent that the defect to its paw was caused by porcupine spines that had become embedded in the pad. Panthers like to eat porcupines and are very astute at killing porcupines without suffering damage from the spines. Why this animal had failed in this respect will never be known, but fail it had and the people of Shirlal and the nearby villages had paid a price in human life!

Chapter 2

The Maneater of the Babur Badans

The Babur Badans or crescent shaped hills are about a hundred and twenty miles to the northwest of Bangalore on the edge of the Western Ghats. The maneater that commenced its operations around the railway station at Athigiri was proof positive that lightning does strike twice. About thirty-five years before my maneater, another tigress had developed the unfortunate habit of chewing its way through the local population. She had been shot by a gentleman called Kenneth Anderson. Mr Anderson died in 1974, but not before he had written several books about his adventures hunting maneaters. They are well worth a read.

The maneater commenced its operations and announced its intention to decimate the local population by taking (in India this is referred to as 'lifting') a railway ganger. The man had been checking the seats or chairs for the rails, about a mile from a tiny halt and group of five railway houses called Bamanavalli. At first, nobody took any great notice of the man's absence, as the work force of India is inclined to take leave of absence whenever they feel the inclination and it was assumed that this was probably the case, but when he failed to return at dusk, it was decided to launch a search the following morning. Following the tracks, the group of searchers eventually found a *chapli*, or country made sandal, at the point where they knew the ganger had been working. Next to the sandal was the hammer that the man had been carrying for the purposes of checking the 'chairs. The ground was very hard, so no tracks were obvious, but eventually somebody noticed a few drops of rust-coloured marks – blood! It never ceased to astound me just how totally inept and ignorant at interpreting signs or in following tracks the average Indian who lives near or in the jungles is. They just do not know the first principles of bush craft! The blood trail was followed to a patch of sand. Here, the group noticed a larger patch of dried blood and next to it, the pug marks of a tiger! At this point, discretion being the better part of valour, the group turned tail and fled. The ganger's body was never found.

Tigers follow a circular route, often, many miles in diameter, called a 'beat'. Eventually, the tiger will revisit a location, usually months after the previous visit. Even after taking to man eating, tigers still follow this habit. This maneater was different because it seemed to favour following the line of the railway with small deviations into the hinterland, the line running from Birur, all the way up to Talguppa, in the far north. Over a period of about six months, the maneater had officially 'lifted' nine victims. In fact, it had probably taken nearly double that number, because in rural India, records are not as accurate as we would expect in the west. One of her victims was a Lumbini poacher. He had climbed on to a low stunted tree and sat on a branch, about six feet above the ground. He was armed with a single barrel, breech loading twelve bores, intending to shoot a deer or a wild pig. Sometime during the night, the maneater came across him, reached up and pulled the man out of the tree. The incident posed a number of questions for me.

Knowing that a maneater was operating in the area, why had he sat on a branch a mere six feet from the ground? This was an act of extreme stupidity! Next, why had he not fired his weapon? At close range, the buckshot would have behaved like a solid bullet and was more than capable of killing a tiger. At the very least, the noise would have frightened the tiger, making it leave the locale. Yet, the cartridge was in the breech, unfired! Fear does terrible things to people, rendering them incapable of defending themselves or taking any form of action. Finally, why had he not tried to climb higher into the tree? Whatever the facts, the poacher had paid a terrible price for his inactivity! Perhaps he had no warning of his fate. The tiger had attacked from the rear, as the claw marks on the tree indicated, and being a mere six feet in the air, the man was well within the tigress's reach without her having to climb the tree. He, probably, never realised he was in danger until the awful moment that the killer grabbed him.

Shortly after my return from hunting the Shirlal maneater, I received a letter from the Permanent Way Inspector at Birur, listing the activities of the maneater and complaining that the animal was doing a very good job of decimating his workforce. The gentleman concluded his missive by begging me to 'shoot the brute!' One factor emerged from the letter; this was the fact that the tiger was tending to operate near a little station or Halt, as we used to call them, in England, in pre-Beeching days. This station did not warrant a name and was some miles from the nearest named settlement of Bamanavalli. I showed the letter to the managing director of the company I was working for, to be told, "Take as much time as you need and shoot the offending cat, such action being considered very good P.R."

The P.W.I., himself, had experienced an unpleasant meeting with the maneater some months earlier. He had been in a group of five men who were checking the track for any damage. The group had stopped for a rest and one of them had climbed a small hillock to smoke a *bedi* or native cigarette, consisting of tobacco wrapped in a betel leaf. Everyone had been resting for a few minutes when, with no warning, a tiger had 'lifted' the lone smoker and, ignoring the man's screams, carried him off, into the surrounding jungle. Everyone in the group ran as fast as possible away from the terrible place.

The local press had a 'Field Day' castigating the P.W.I. as an errant coward for deserting the ganger in his hour of need. The P.W.I. was unarmed, so how was he supposed to react to the situation? I wonder how many of those who called the poor man a coward, or worse, would have reacted any differently, if they had been there? I, for one, would have been running with the best!

I travelled by train from Bangalore, alighting at Bamanavalli at about 15:30. I found the journey quite amusing, as I believe that nowhere in the world, except India, can a white man be carrying a rifle travel on a train without causing so much as a raised eyebrow! Not once was I questioned about my reasons or intentions.

Calling at the station master's office, I showed him the letter from the P.W.I. The station master promised his full cooperation and, more importantly, offered me a room on the station platform for my personal use. It did not take me long to make myself at home. Having eaten my evening meal, I sat on the edge of my camp-bed and cleaned my new rifle, a double-barrelled weapon made by Rigby of Edinburgh and chambered for the 470 Nitro express cartridge. A real cat stoppers! I nicknamed the rifle 'Daisy-May'. The right barrel was called 'Daisy' and the left barrel was called 'May' and that rifle was to be my comfort and companion on many of my misadventures. Apart from a couple of passing trains that did not stop, I had a peaceful night.

I spent the next few days investigating various suggestions made by the local populace as to the tiger's possible location, but apart from being told that I was looking for a very large tiger, I gained nothing from the exercise. At one point, I found a small pool of water – it had the pug marks of a largish and rather elderly tigress in the mud at the water's edge, her age being gauged by the degree to which her pads and claws had splayed out. As the big cats age, their pads and claws tend to splay out and become quite rutted across the pads. I had been told that the killer was a tiger, so I dismissed my findings as irrelevant. Experience would ensure that I did not make that mistake again! To the average Indian villager, all tigers are around fifteen feet in length and are male and weigh about 1000 pounds! The reality is that any tiger over ten feet is huge and probably weighs between 450 lbs and 500 lbs. When asked about size, the average Indian will stretch out his arms, wide, and tell you that the tiger's head was that big. This is obviously a gross exaggeration, but I cannot see any change taking place in this appraisal of the size of a tiger. A tigress is smaller and often weighs between 250 lbs and 350 lbs on average. I was looking at the pug marks of the killer, as I was to find out later.

It would be a pointless exercise to give a day-by-day account of my search for the maneater. Suffice to say that I had a hot and dusty time chasing the tiger's tail. After one particularly hot day, I had a cold shower from the station water tank and then settled down to sleep. I was awakened with a start by an ear-splitting scream. I jumped off the camp bed, pulled my trousers and boots on and then put my bush-jacket on followed by my hat. All this took just a couple of minutes. Exiting my little room, I grabbed my rifle and a couple of spare rounds and trotted out on to the platform. I met the station master and a porter who told me that they thought the scream that everyone had heard had emanated from a hut at the side of the track about half a mile away from the station. This open-fronted shed provided shelter for the railway gangers during the monsoon season, when it can get very wet.

The time was about 02:30 am. The moon was by no means a full moon, but the sky was relatively cloudless so that I could see, clearly, for about thirty yards. I set off to find the source of the scream that had rudely disturbed my slumbers. I found the hut and noticed with a rather grim satisfaction that there was a pool of blood in front of the open doorway. I asked myself the very obvious question of what sort of an idiot would sleep outside with a maneater on the prowl? Slowly and carefully, I began to follow the blood trail, taking very great care to check any bush or even a blade of grass that could conceal a killer. At night, a blood trail shows up as a series of virtually black splashes, on whatever it lands on. The trail ran along a game path that almost touched the back of the hut. After about half an hour, I had covered about 250 yards when I noticed an object, about the size of a football, sat in the middle of the game path. Very carefully, with my rifle at the ready and my thumb on the safety catch and my finger down the outside of the trigger guard, I walked up to the object and discovered that it was a human head! The killer had obviously bitten the head off, but why? Closer inspection provided the answer. The head was from someone in the last stages of Leprosy! The affliction that everyone in the sub-continent lives in dread of catching, native and European, alike. Europeans can afford the drugs that will stop Leprosy, but most Indians cannot afford such luxury and, so, they live with the consequences of the infection. A consequence that will lead to a slow, agonising, lingering death. My macabre discovery answered a lot of questions. Obviously, the poor man had been in terrible pain and discomfort, and having been shunned by his fellow man, he had hidden himself by the hut, perhaps he had deliberately chosen death by maneater rather than endure any more suffering, we will never know! Why had the man screamed if his intention was to die? If you were being attacked by a maneater, whatever your intentions, I suspect you would utter an involuntary scream!

A little further along, I found the pug marks of the killer in a patch of soft sand. They were the pug marks of a large tigress, well past her prime. I continued to track her for about a mile until the tracks disappeared on the baked ground. I could go no further. Slowly, I retreated, noting that the breeze was coming from behind me and that any attack would come from my front. Arriving back at the station, I filled the station master in on events and my discoveries, flopped on to my camp bed and fell asleep. Next morning, accompanied by a couple of trackers, I found what was left of the body. Apart from a few bones, the answer was nothing. A small fire was built, and the few remaining bones burnt to ash. When the ashes had cooled, they were scattered in a nearby stream as

Hindu custom required, so that they could find their way into the Ganges. Hindus believe that in order to be born again, their ashes have to be cast into the Ganga Ma (Mother Ganges) or a stream or river that will run into the Ganges. The ashes are carried out to sea and the Hindu is reborn in another life and so the cycle of birth, life, death, and rebirth is continued.

Three days later, a ganger was taken, at dusk, when he was lighting the signal lamps for the halt. These lights consist of an inner light and an outer light. On being told that the ganger had failed to return and that the station master feared the worst, I set off along the track, walking on the same side of the rails as the signal lamps, to find the missing ganger. I found the inner signal lamp. It was lit. I continued on and found the outer signal lamp was also lit. This indicated that the man had been taken on the way back, after completing his duties! I started to walk very slowly along the track, towards the station. This time, I walked on the opposite side of the track to the one I had walked on, as I walked up the line. I had not walked very far when I found traces of blood on the gravel base of the lines, but nothing to indicate the direction taken by the blood donor. A little further on, I came across a culvert that ran under the line. The culvert was about fifteen feet high and about twelve feet in length. About fifteen feet from the end of the culvert was a dark shape. I had a good look around for signs of any problems and then I climbed down the embankment, and very carefully, approached the object that had attracted my attention, and on examination, found that the bundle was the body of the missing ganger, marinating in its own blood. The cadaver had, very obviously, been killed by a tiger. The reason I did not find it on my way up was quite simple. I had been walking on the other side of the banking,

43

so the corpse had been hidden from my view. I pushed the safety up on the 470 and had a careful look around me. There was no sign of the maneater. It is not unknown for maneaters to kill a victim, leave the body, then return later to feed. Equally, she may have been in hiding watching my every move. A comforting thought? No, I don't think so! And one guaranteed to give you a feeling of great inferiority! However, to return to the business of the day, if the tigress returned, I would be waiting for her, but where?

There was no place to build a *machan*, nor was there a suitable tree to climb or bush to hide behind. My only hope, it seemed to me, was to lay on the tracks that crossed the culvert. If the cat tried to stalk me, I would hear her on the very loose gravel that formed the embankment. On that basis, I could deal with her long before she got too close! The culvert was too high for the tigress to attempt a vertical leap of some fifteen feet – remember, after all, she was an old animal. So, I was safe from surprise attack. The moon was about threequarters full and there were few clouds in the sky, so I had plenty of light to shoot by. I settled down to await the return of the killer, by resting my body on a sleeper. My body was just inside the rails and my feet were just over the end of the rails, dangling in space. I had been laid there for about three hours when, with no warning whatsoever, there was a loud snarl behind me followed by a scratching, followed by a heavy thud. I sat bolt upright and realised that the maneater had attempted what I had believed to be impossible, a vertical leap of fifteen feet and she had missed grabbing my feet, quite literally, by inches! Being new to maneater hunting, I had failed to register that the animal and bird life in the surrounding jungle had gone very quiet. Had I noticed the silence, it would have warned me that the tigress was nearby. This was a lesson I learned and a mistake I never repeated. Even now, I am still surprised that an elderly tigress could attempt a vertical leap of fifteen feet from a standing start and very nearly make it! I spent the rest of that long night sat on a sleeper, in the middle of the culvert with the 470 across my knees! As I expected, the tigress had gone and did not return. As dawn broke, I walked back to the halt and recounted my adventures. Taking a party of men with me I returned to the culvert, and we collected the body of the dead ganger so that it could be handed to the man's relatives for cremation.

To recount the next fourteen days, blow by blow, would be very boring and a waste of your time, gentle reader. I seemed to be doing nothing but chasing shadows, something you do a lot of when hunting a maneater, as I came to learn. I spent my days walking the game trails looking for fresh pug marks (tiger tracks). I was returning from a day's walking and was about fifty yards from the halt, when I heard voices talking loudly and the sound of a woman's voice crying and sobbing. Most unusual, to say the least!

As I walked around a gentle bend and into view of the Halt, the station master saw me, and everyone ran towards me. The woman who was crying, ran up to me and flung her arms around my legs and would not let go of me. Sadly, I no-longer have this sort of effect on young women, a handicap of aging, I believe. I handed my unloaded rifle to one of the men and bending down, I gently prised the woman from around my legs, all the while she was sobbing. "Save Harjinder, save my son, *Sahib*."

I asked for an account of what had happened. It transpired that the woman's son, Harjinder – age eleven – had gone out with three others and a flock of goats so that the goats could graze in the jungle. A tiger had appeared from nowhere, and in the ensuing melee, one of the men in the group had seen the tiger seize the boy. The men, wisely, did not hang around and they fled to the station, to find the *sahib* who was hunting for the killer.

Retrieving my rifle, I sent the group back to the halt. I, then, started to follow the tracks of the flock so that I could find the place where the attack had occurred. After tracking for about a mile, I found the place where the attack had taken place. The large pool of blood confirmed my worst fears because, any human body that had produced that amount of blood was assuredly dead and beyond any help that I could render. Fortunately, because the blood trail was so prolific, tracking was relatively easy, apart from the need to watch the surrounding bushes to guard against any attack. The breeze was coming from my left at about eight o'clock and so any attack would come from my right-hand side.

Before long, I came upon what was left of Harjinder. The tigress had eaten a good meal and had left just a few bones and the skull. The jungle was very quiet, not a bird call or the screaming of the langur monkeys broke the silence, indicating quite clearly that the killer was nearby. But, surrounded as I was on all sides by dense bush and scrub, I did not know where! Other than the fact that the breeze was constant, so it was highly likely that any attack would come from my right. The bird life and the langurs were not going to help, because they had gone very quiet. I do so hate it when the jungle goes quiet, it inevitably means trouble for the *shikari*, hunter! I emptied the pockets of my bush jacket, putting the spare rounds for the 470 in my trouser pocket. I wrapped the pitiful

46

remains of Harjinder in my jacket and set off back to the halt. There was no point in sitting over the body and waiting for the tiger to resume its meal, because the tigress had not left enough to warrant a return visit. The killer knew where I was and would, without a doubt, not return until I had gone. On reaching the halt, my jacket and its contents were taken away by the villagers. Later, I could smell the cremation fire as I ate my evening meal and assumed that my jacket had been incinerated, after all it was soaked in blood. Imagine my surprise when my jacket arrived next morning clean and ready to wear! How the ladies of the village had done it, I do not know, but I was very grateful to get my jacket back.

About three days later, just about midday, on a bright and sunny summer's day, a woodcutter was taken by the tiger. The men with him ran to the halt to give me the news, as they knew I was living at the station. Luckily, I was just having lunch. I grabbed my new 470 and set off to follow the trail. I was shown the place where the man had been taken. I sent the men back to the halt as I could not guarantee their safety if they accompanied me. When dealing with a maneater, it is often enough of a problem looking to your own safety without having to look to the welfare of others. After all, they might get in the way of you shooting the offending killer, or they could be mauled before you can do anything about the situation. For these reasons I have always hunted alone, except once, when hunting the Mysore Maneater. I followed the trail for about four hundred yards, at which point it entered a nullah or dry river/stream bed. I started to follow, but quickly realised I was potentially committing suicide, because the maneater would have all the advantages. It could attack me from behind or in front. It could attack from the banks of the nullah, about two feet above my head. Never, never, follow a maneater up a nullah on your own. If you attempt it, then make sure your will is made out. Your solicitor will need it, virtually certainly! I retreated slowly to the entrance of the nullah and reviewed the situation.

The plan I hatched was quite simple. I decided that I would do a detour and enter the nullah well above where I thought the maneater would be, and I would use the shadow cast by the banks of the nullah to my advantage. It was a bright summer's day without a cloud in the sky, so I would not have to worry about clouds hiding the sun. I did a detour of about half a mile and carefully looked around for any sign of the tiger. There was no evidence of the animal, so I slowly and silently slid over the edge of the nullah. I examined the soft bed of the nullah, the soft sand revealed no evidence of the maneater. Keeping close to one bank I used the shadow of the bank to indicate if anything was above me, if it was, I would see the outline of the nullah move and that was something it should not do! I could watch in front of me and the top of the far bank of the nullah, for any sign of the maneater. There was very little chance of a sneak attack. Slowly, I edged down the nullah. Ahead was a bend going away to my right. I stopped, and breaking the 470 open, I checked to make sure 'Daisy-May' was loaded. It was fine, so I started to edge forward, and I had taken about a dozen paces when the maneater stepped around the bend with her victim in her mouth. On seeing me, the tigress dropped the body and snarling, she crouched down with her head almost touching the bed of the nullah. Her rear was stuck up in the air with her tail stood on end, rigid. The position of the tail was a sure indication that she was about to launch her attack. I picked a spot just behind her head, aiming to break the spine, and fired Daisy. The bullet took her exactly as I wanted it to, breaking her spine. I walked forward until I was about nine feet away and fired May into the top of her head, completely destroying the brain pan! Golden rule: always pay the insurance. I have seen what happens when a 'dead' maneater gets up and starts chewing people. It's messy!

Examination of the tigress proved what I had suspected. She was an animal well past her prime. Her teeth were worn away and her claws were splayed and bushed out. She must have found hunting her normal prey increasingly difficult and presumably this is why she had taken to hunting the easiest game, man.

Chapter 3

The Lame Horror of Palibonu

If ever there was a cautionary tale of the effects of human interference on wild animals, then this is that tale.

Palibonu is a small village about 100 miles southwest of Bangalore. Its troubles began when a largish tiger descended the hills of the Nilgiris and took up residence near the village. The reasons for this strange behaviour soon became apparent, as the animal started by taking cattle that were being grazed in the surrounding forests. No doubt the tiger had reasoned that it was far easier to hunt slow-and dim-witted cattle, rather than try to hunt the worldly-wise game of the forests. As the toll of cattle began to grow, the villagers, who being very poor, could ill afford to lose any of their beasts, moved the cattle closer to the village. Not unnaturally, the tiger decided to follow his meals on the hoof, to the village.

Eventually, the tiger took a step too far. It killed and carried off a large black bull owned by the village *patel* (headman). This man swore vengeance and retribution against the *shaitan* (devil) that had taken his prized bull and had given affront to his exalted status as headman. He had in his shed a ferocious looking Gin trap that measured about eighteen inches across and in Victorian times was called a mantrap and was used, in England, against poachers. Accompanied by two men, the *patel* set off to find the kill. They found the dead bull and artfully concealed the trap near the carcase of the kill and disappeared back to the village to await results.

Eventually, the tiger returned to its kill, and in resuming his meal, he triggered the trap. The vicious teeth closed around his right leg with frightening speed. The tiger was trapped. He roared for hours, but nobody was brave enough to try to kill the tiger despite the presence in the village of a shotgun and two muzzle loaders. Sometime during the night, the tiger managed to tear its leg free from the trap and limp off into the jungle in very great pain, disappearing into the vast forests of the Nilgiris, apparently, never to be seen or heard from again. Everyone breathed a sigh of relief and thanked the *patel* for his timely intervention. However, this situation of tranquillity did not last. After a lapse of about six months, the tiger reappeared, but there was an important difference in his attitude. The easy going, if obnoxious, cattle lifter was gone, and in its place was a tiger that had become that most terrible of scourges, a maneater. Its leg had been so badly injured by the gin trap that it, now, found hunting its normal prey very difficult and so it took to hunting man!

The first kill took place about twelve miles from Palibonu. The victim was a herdsman who had driven his herd into the forest to graze. When the unfortunate man failed to return for his evening meal, his eldest son and a few friends set out to look for him. Eventually, they found the herd scattered over a large area and grazing peacefully with no sign of the missing herdsman. As the group was rounding up the cattle, one of the numbers noticed a largish patch of drying blood. At this point, nobody assumed anything wrong, instead it was assumed that the missing man had injured himself in an accident. However, as they followed the trail of blood, somebody noticed the pug marks of a largish tiger. At this point, the group decided that discretion was the better part of valour and they beat a hasty retreat! The body of the herdsman was never found. The average Indian takes the view that it is pointless to risk your life trying to find somebody who is already dead. An argument that is difficult to reason against.

During his career of man eating, the Lame Tiger of Palibonu was credited with a total of nineteen victims during his six-month reign of terror. It averaged three kills per month, suggesting that although its hunting ability was seriously impaired, it was still able to hunt game in the forests.

Shortly after it had killed it's seventeenth victim, I received a letter from the District Forestry Officer (D.F.O) asking for my help in shooting the tiger. Accordingly, I obtained leave of absence from my superiors, packed my gear into my jeep and headed off for Palibonu. On arrival at the village, I met the headman, who told me all about the tiger, including, with remarkable honesty, his part in the creation of the maneater. I pitched my tent under a Banyan tree on the outskirts of the village and had a talk to the villagers. It appeared that the tiger never entered a village in pursuit of a meal. Instead, it preferred to take its victims in the forests. I was told that I would have no problem identifying the animal because of its very definite limp. It's pug marks showing as three pugs with a furrow like marking where it could not use its off-fore paw. Using this information, I spent about a week walking the various game trails looking for the distinctive pugs in any soft earth. During this period, I had seen the killer's pugs on a couple of occasions, but the tracks were very obviously weeks old.

Early one morning, a message arrived, brought by three men armed with a rusty sword, a spear, and a muzzle loading musket, these weapons being for protection. They had come from a hamlet about five miles away and they told me that a woman had gone out to collect water from a stream when she had been 'lifted' by the maneater, an event witnessed by three women who were nearby. The track to the hamlet was so bad that it was impassable, even to my jeep, so I set off and walked the five miles arriving at about midday. I was given directions to the stream but refused offers to show me the way. If I got into an argument with our limping feline, I did not want the worry of having others with me. Arriving at the stream, I eventually found the spot where the woman was killed. Slowly, I tracked the blood trail and I had covered about a mile in just over an hour. It was autumn and I noticed that the light was just starting to fail, so I made my way back to the hamlet. The question was where to spend the night. I, eventually, decided on a cattle barn. Covering myself in straw and surrounded by cattle that would warn me of any approach by the tiger, I fell asleep. I got up at dawn and had a breakfast of tea and chapattis supplied by members of the hamlet. I set off to take up the trail of the maneater. I found where the tiger had originally left the cadaver but noticed with grim satisfaction that the animal had returned in the night and had removed the body. Perhaps if I had sat up in a nearby tree, I might have shot the maneater, but I had failed to find the body before dark set in. The body was never found, as the blood trail petered out and the pug marks could not be seen on the concrete hard ground. Feeling very frustrated I returned to the hamlet.

The headman of the hamlet suggested that I might like to tie out two or three buffaloes as bait. I don't like using live animals as bait as I feel the animals know, only too well, what fate awaits them. I was glad, therefore, that during the course of a week; not one of the three buffaloes was touched. I gave up on the buffaloes, when a goatherd near Palibonu was taken when he was guarding his flock. Despite knowing about the maneater, the man had, unwisely, walked close to a dense growth of bush. As he passed the bushes, he had been 'lifted' by the cat. On receiving this news, I packed my small bag with a pullover, flask of tea, and some food.

Arriving at the area where the kill had taken place I, eventually, found evidence of the kill. I tracked the tiger, following pug marks and blood spots, to the point where it had left the partially eaten cadaver. Not more than twenty yards away was a Ficus tree. I could, hopefully, sit on one of its lower branches and await the return of the maneater. I chose a branch about fifteen feet from the ground. Normally, this might be considered a little low for safety, but I reasoned that the tiger, incapacitated by its damaged limb, would find it very difficult to climb the tree and would most assuredly make a lot of noise in the process and would allow me plenty of time to give the brute a permanent cure for migraine. During the afternoon, the tree was visited by a variety of birds. My lack of movement did not frighten them, and that same lack of movement would not betray my presence to the maneater. The cadaver was covered in flies, and though I have virtually no sense of smell, even I could detect the sweet greenish odour of a decaying corpse. A corpse has a very strong and unpleasant odour, so I am told.

As the sun started to drop behind the Western Ghats, the temperature started to drop, so I took the opportunity to put my pullover on under my bush jacket, eat a chapatti and drink some tea, but not too much tea, as wanting to answer the call of nature is not a good idea when sitting up for a maneater! Settling down to watch, I noticed that the jungle had gone very quiet, with no bird sound or the call of the Langur monkeys in evidence – this was not a good sign as this silence would tend to indicate the presence, nearby, of a big cat! I had been sat for some hours; the semi-diameter moon had risen and was giving a soft light, so that I could make out the cadaver when I heard a gentle sigh coming from the other side of the corpse and near some scrub. The tiger had returned! I did not move a muscle. I sat absolutely motionless, then came an ominous growl from the direction of the scrub. I had been rumbled!

Finding that the growl had no effect on me, the tiger began to roar, repeatedly, and circle the tree; taking good care to stay out of sight. The roars were intended to unnerve me and make me jump out of the tree and run away – exposing me to attack, in the process. The roars had the opposite effect, because I knew exactly where the killer was and I was confident that if he tried to climb the tree with his impaired limb, I would have plenty of time to place one and a half ounces of nickel jacketed 470 exactly where I wanted it. The roars were changing, I could tell from the timbre of the calls that the maneater was working himself up to attack the tree. Finally with the unmistakable 'woof, woof', he charged the tree. I had chosen a spot where two thick branches formed a V for me to sit on. I stood up on the V. The tiger was behind me, scrabbling at the trunk in his efforts to climb the tree and reach me. I leant around the trunk and raised the 470 to my shoulder, pushing the safety up to the 'fire' position. As his body came into view, the tiger fell out of the tree and on landing on the ground, without hesitation, he bolted for cover. In a heartbeat, he was gone. Even a three-legged tiger can move very quickly. He obligingly roared his displeasure at how events had turned out and I could follow his departing progress for a couple of miles.

Having no reason now to deny myself, I had another chapatti, a drink of tea, and settled down to smoke my pipe. Dawn arrived and having satisfied myself that the tiger had not returned and was waiting for me to descend the tree – the birds were calling, and the Langurs were busy swearing at a panther about half a mile away, I climbed down and relieved the severe ache in my derriere – Ouch!

Some parts of the Western Ghats are covered in dense Sal forests. The Sal tree has a variety of uses when cut down, including use as railway sleepers. For this reason foresting of the Sal takes place on a regular basis. To facilitate this, camps are created to house two or three dozen woodcutters. The accommodation is usually bamboo huts, with a lattice style wall with a space of about twelve inches around the base in an effort to prevent the local ants from munching their way through the bamboo of the huts. It was July and the oppressive heat of the summer was starting to ease, so the huts were quite comfy. Everything was fine, the woodcutters were chopping down the Sal and were living quite happily in the camps. At this juncture, the maneater decided to throw the proverbial spanner in the works.

The camps were about fifteen miles from Palibonu and had been unmolested and untroubled by the activities of the three-legged assassin that was operating further to the east.

However, this situation changed in grand fashion. The killer decided to pay one of the camps a late-night visit! Why? When it had a reputation for never entering a village, when looking for a victim, I do not know. The killer hauled a woodcutter out of a hut by the simple expedient of putting its good paw under the wall, sinking its claws into the man's shoulder and dragging him clear of the hut before carrying the man off, still kicking and screaming. His friends had the somewhat dubious privilege of listening to the man's cries of pain and pleas for help, as the poor man was carried off into the vast Sal forests.

Next morning, at daybreak, the D.F.O. (District Forestry Officer) sent three men to carry a message to me. The note explained what had happened and closed by asking for my help, as the woodcutters were threatening to depart for healthier climes. Initially, I thought that the killer must be another tiger, but the note made the emphatic point that the killer had only three good legs. Thinking about the situation, I realised that fifteen miles could be walked by the tiger in less than three hours and that the walk would, probably, only serve to develop the killer's appetite.

The runners had arrived at about nine o'clock, as I had just finished breakfast and was wondering why I had heard of no more kills. The reason for my lack of information was now obvious. I put the men in my jeep, together with spare clothes and my rifle. We set off along the forest tracks and we arrived at the camp from which the man had been taken at about eleven o'clock. I started to question the men, who were rightly terrified and refusing to emerge from their huts. The woodcutters pointed out the direction taken by the maneater, so I set off to follow the track followed by the killer. Soon after leaving the camp, I found the blood trail and started to follow the cat. The maneater had gone into the depths of the Sal forest and in the dense undergrowth, tracking was far from easy. Eventually, led by the blood spoor, I found the place in a shallow nullah where the maneater had consumed his grisly meal. Apart from some very small splinters of bone, there was nothing left. The hyenas, jackals, and other scavengers had cleared everything the killer had left.

I stood for a while, trying to decide which way the cat had gone. I decided that in all probability, the killer had most likely followed the nullah up the hillside. Why I thought this, I do not know, but sometimes you just have to go with your gut feeling. I set off up the nullah, it was only about two feet in depth, and I am well aware of what I said about pursuing a maneater up a nullah when hunting the Maneater of the Babur Badans, but this had to be done and the nullah was very shallow, allowing me to see along the top of the nullah and the surrounding shrubbery. I was taking very great care to examine every boulder, clump of grass, or bush that could hide a killer, at the same time I checked the wind to make sure the breeze was on my back. I had made steady progress for about an hour and had reached the point where the nullah ceased. I was studying the ground in an effort to try to find any sort of indication of which way the killer had gone. My mental processes were disturbed by Langur monkeys calling in alarm from about half a mile ahead. I knew, with absolute certainty from the noise they were making, that they had sighted a big cat. I broke the 470 open and checked the two rounds in the chambers, then I worked the safety catch a couple of times to make sure it was moving smoothly. It's not nice to have a firearms malfunction when faced with a homicidal cat. Having carried out the checks, I started to walk towards the Langurs to find out what had given them a dose of hysterics! Langurs are prone to having a dose of hysterics when they see a member of the family Felidae. It is a very useful indication to the *shikari*, that trouble might not be too far away.

Walking on the outsides of my feet, in an effort to make no sound, I started to creep forward, when after a couple of minutes I noticed that a family of Langurs had started calling from behind me! They could not see me, but something had spooked them. I noted that a gentle breeze was blowing from my rear. The awful thought occurred about the possibility of the killer circling around and could, now, be stalking me from the rear! As these far from pleasant thoughts passed through my head, I hid behind the trunk of a large Sal and waited. Less than a minute later, three men emerged from the Sal, following in my footsteps. I stood up and signalled them to be quiet and to come to me as quickly as possible. I asked the men what they thought they were doing, blundering about with a maneater on the prowl. I was informed that they were looking for the body of the dead man, so that they could cremate the cadaver. I rather tersely informed them that there was nothing left to cremate!

Knowing that in all probability there was a maneater half a mile ahead, my major problem was what to do with the three woodcutters, if I was to continue tracking the killer. I, certainly, could not take the men with me. My problem was brought to a head, when a family of Langurs about two hundred yards ahead started calling in alarm, closely followed by a Chital hind uttering her scream of alarm. Everything was suggesting that the tiger was closing, presumably to find out what all the commotion was about, further down the hill. Looking around I noticed a clump of bushes crowded together. I made the men sit behind me in the clump. Under different circumstances, the looks on their faces, of abject fear, would have been amusing, but not at this point in time! I knelt down on one knee, so that I was largely concealed by the shrubbery, and faced the direction that I knew the maneater would probably approach from and awaited events.

After about ten minutes, an awfully long time when you are expecting a visit from a homicidal tiger, I noticed that the undergrowth about twenty yards away moved gently, could this be caused by the breeze? As I was considering this possibility, a tiger's head emerged from the undergrowth. I, very quietly and slowly, raised the 470 to my shoulder, aligning the foresight with the vee of the rear sight on the tiger's head, just above an imaginary line drawn between the eyes. I started to squeeze the trigger, when with no warning, one of the men cannoned into my elbow, as I fired. This caused the rifle to slew around sufficiently to miss the tiger, who, being a complete bounder did not wait for me to fire the second barrel, instead, he scarpered into the crud! To say that my language was a trifle colourful would be an understatement. As a result of playing rugby, I was very fluent in 'Anglo Saxon', causing the man to explain that he had been trying to get a better view of my killing the tiger, when he had slipped and crashed into me. Under the circumstances, I did not have the heart to shout at the man again, nor to point out that his actions had probably cost the lives of more people. He was only too aware of what he had done and looked as though he would like the ground to open up and swallow him! However, one of his colleagues had no such qualms. He launched a vicious attack, kicking and punching the poor man, until I stepped in and stopped the aggressor. It was a long walk back to camp and the gentleman who had been rather free with his fists and feet, took every opportunity to castigate and berate the elbow jogging miscreant.

During the next couple of weeks, the limping tiger took three more victims. I spent a lot of time trying to track the victims, but usually lost the trail on hard ground down by the river. On one occasion, I spent seven hours tracking a blood trail and pug marks, before the trail petered out. The undergrowth was very dense, and it is rather trying on the nerves, to have to negotiate such cover, never knowing when or if the maneater was going to attack! It never becomes easy, but the more you do this, the more relaxed about it and confident in your own abilities you become.

I revisited the logging camp and whilst having a drink of tea with the loggers, one of them asked if I was aware that the limping tiger was in the habit of walking along the nearby river. Nobody had ever mentioned this piece of intelligence, don't ask me why not, I don't know. I should explain that in the monsoon season, the river was about a hundred yards wide and impassable to foot traffic, but during the present dry season the river was a mere trickle a few yards wide with extensive banks of white sand. Here was an opportunity that I could not turn down! The men assured me that it was the three-legged tiger, because of the tracks he left. I calculated that I had about an hour of daylight left, so decided to visit the river to have a look. Arriving at the river, I noticed a fallen tree stump, virtually in the middle of the dry riverbed. I noticed with some satisfaction, that one side of the stump had a large number of tracks, all made by a three-legged tiger. I had dressed for the night and so I had no excuses for not waiting for our limping feline. I settled in among the huge roots to await events. The night closed in and I settled down to a long vigil. I listened carefully to the sounds of the jungle in the hope that I might get some warning of impending danger. In fact, the local wildlife continued to chatter, unabated. The moon, which was nearly full, kept disappearing behind the scudding clouds that were being driven by a stiff breeze. Between the periods of darkness the sand was lit up by the moon.

During one of the periods of darkness, I noticed that I had been sat motionless for a couple of hours, when for no reason that I could determine, the hairs on the back of my neck stood on end. The sixth sense that we all possess was telling me that I was in great danger, but where from? At the same time I noted that the local wildlife had stopped chattering and I noticed with an almost detached curiosity that my hands had suddenly become very sweaty. During all the time that I had been sat in the tree roots, I had been moving my head gently and slowly from side to side. Now, as I turned my head, I was convinced that I saw a shadow on the riverbed about thirty yards away and I was certain that the shadow had not been there before! As I continued to watch, I was sure that the shadow had moved and then, had moved again. Then I realised that it was the maneater and it was creeping towards me in short bursts of movement! I raised the 470 and pushed the safety to its 'fire' position. The maneater must have seen the slight movement. It stopped and the shadow became shorter, and I knew that the cat was preparing to charge. I aimed at the shadow about twenty yards away and squeezed the trigger. At the report, all hell broke loose! The tiger roared, leapt up and clawed the air, before falling back to the riverbed, then it started to shuffle towards me, pulling itself along on its front legs, with its back legs trailing behind. I fired again, at a range of about fifteen yards. Still the brute kept coming! The thought passed through my mind that I must be firing marsh mellows! I reloaded with the two spare rounds from between the fingers of my left hand. By now, the tiger was about nine feet away. I fired through its open mouth, dropping the animal stone dead as one and a half ounces of nickel jacketed lead smashed its brains to a pulp.

Having satisfied myself that the maneater was dead, I sat down on the stump and lit my pipe. During the night a herd of elephants came down to the river to drink and bathe. They scented the dead tiger and stampeded away screaming shrilly! It would appear that even dead tigers have the facility to frighten and intimidate other residents of the jungle.

Finally, the dawn broke in the east and shortly after, a group of woodcutters appeared. They had heard my three shots and they had come to see if I was all right. Very brave and very kind of them, as they had no way of knowing that the killer was dead. The men cut down a sapling and having fastened the tiger to it, carried the maneater back to my jeep.

I took the carcase to the D.F.O., who had the tiger skinned. We found that in the pitch black of night, my shooting had not been at fault. My first shot had gone through its open mouth and had smashed the spine, a little far back, but definitely a stopper and causing the animal to drag itself towards me on its front legs. My second shot had gone through the chest, taking out the heart and lungs. Only adrenaline had kept the brute moving, until my final shot had smashed the brain rendering adrenaline useless.

The lame maneater of Palibonu had killed a total of nineteen people, it would kill no more!

Chapter 4

The Vallarander Maneater

Vallarander is a largish village, about seventy miles south west of Bangalore – Bangalore is, now, known as Bengaluru. Take the road south towards Ootacumund and Segur and before reaching Ooty, take the Ghat road up the dip slope of the Nilgiris to reach your destination. Vallarander is surrounded by a number of large tea plantations, one of these was owned by a man called Mangal Thrapur. Typical of many tea planters, he had shot various game and a few panthers, but had never shot a tiger. He decided that he needed to correct this omission, accordingly, he put the word out, in the surrounding villages, that if anyone reported a tiger kill, they would be well rewarded. Soon, it was reported that a buffalo had been killed, not far from the village. A local *shikari* – native hunter – arranged for a *machan* to be constructed in a tree overlooking the kill. Thrapur and the *shikari* took their places in the *machan*, well before dusk. Why Thrapur needed someone to babysit him is not clear, after all, you are far better sitting up alone, when shooting a big cat; rather than have a companion with you and being tempted to talk to them. Thrapur was armed with a 30.06 Springfield, a very efficient weapon and adequate tiger stopper, if used properly. The tiger returned just before sunset, when the light was still perfectly adequate for shooting. Giving the tiger time to settle to his meal, about the only sensible thing he did that night, Thrapur fired and hit the tiger, but too far back to do any real damage to the spine or other vital parts. Instead, the bullet passed through the tiger's body and ploughed into the ground. On receiving the bullet, the tiger reportedly roared, very loudly – I'll bet it did! The tiger then, bolted for the undergrowth, before Thrapur could work the bolt of his rifle and fire a second shot.

When I spoke to the *shikari* later, he told me that the jungle went very quiet after the shot and remained that way. He, of all people, should have known that this silence betokened the fact that the tiger had not run off, but was still in the immediate vicinity. Because of this, what they did next was incredibly stupid and the *shikari* should have known better! The *shikari* and Thrapur sat for over two hours but heard and saw nothing. Thrapur decided he preferred a nice warm bed, to sitting on an uncomfortable *machan*, so they climbed down and set off for Thrapur's car, parked up about three miles away. Neither man seemed to attach any significance to the overwhelming silence that engulfed them. Ignorant pair of idiots! The *shikari*, in particular, was displaying an ignorance or ineptitude that I feel, even all these years later, was total incompetence and implied that he was not fit to pursue the calling of *shikari*. They had walked for about a mile, with the *shikari* in the lead. As they passed an area of denser vegetation, the tiger launched its attack with the characteristic 'wroof, wroof'. The tiger charged and leapt on the man at the rear, Thrapur. A single bite to the neck ensured that Thrapur felt no pain after the first bite. During all this commotion, the *shikari* took to his heels and fled, despite the fact that he was carrying a shotgun. Why didn't he fire the gun? When the *shikari* eventually reached the local police station, he reported what had happened. The police were very sceptical about the account, but nonetheless set off accompanied by the *shikari* to find the body. The three policemen were armed with single shot Lee-Enfields. The magazine having being removed from the rifle so that some trigger-happy constable cannot re-enact Davy Crockett's last stand at the Alamo, or whatever! Thrapur was found where he had fallen, the tiger had not touched him beyond the first fatal bite.

Three days after Thrapur's untimely demise, Police Inspector Ramish Gopar called to see me early in the morning. My bearer, Govind, showed the inspector into the study and as I was eating breakfast in the breakfast room, came to inform me that I had a visitor. Walking into the study, I greeted Ram, who responded, "Jock, just have a look at these photographs, please." The photographs confirmed the *shikari*'s account of how the late Mr Thrapur had met his untimely end. They gave a very convincing pictorial demonstration of death by tiger. Ram then asked me what the likelihood was that the tiger could turn maneater. Based on the evidence, I suggested that the possibility was less than fifty percent, based on the fact that the tiger had not eaten any part of Thrapur. All the evidence suggested that the animal was simply taking revenge on the man who had hurt it. I got that one wrong, didn't I? However, two things struck me as being very unusual. Firstly, having been shot the animal did not run away, most animals would run away and hide making following up, in the case of a tiger, a very precarious activity. Instead, this tiger had followed the two men and awaited a chance to take its revenge. Secondly, the animal had made no attempt to attack the *shikari*, presumably it felt that it had inflicted sufficient retribution on Thrapur.

I suggested to Ram that the tiger did not appear to be too badly hurt and would probably recover from its wounds. Therefore, the police should let everyone in the area know that a tiger had been wounded and that care should be taken when working in the forests. Ram agreed with my suggestion and when he left, he took my promise that if the tiger killed, again, I would take all steps to shoot the animal.

A fortnight passed and nothing was heard of the tiger, then it made its second kill. A woman from Vallarander was cutting wood with some other women from the village. The woman who was about to die approached a fallen tree. The tiger was hiding behind the fallen trunk. It was hungry and angry and in pain. As soon as the woman drew near to the fallen tree, the tiger killed her. As it was killing the woman, the other women ran off. Maybe it was the sight of blood, or the smell of blood, or even the taste of blood as it was killing the woman, but for whatever reason the tiger ate part of the woman's lower back and buttocks. Liking the taste, at this point, a maneater was born. Ram called to see me the day after the woman was killed and as agreed, I set off for Vallarander carrying an order from Ram to the local police to give me every assistance. I arrived at about three in the afternoon and made camp, pitching my tent in a grove in a Banyan plantation and surrounding the tent with a thorn barrier. Next, I chatted with the villagers about the kill. One of the women averred that the tiger appeared to have no physical problems when killing the woman. Following the directions given to me by the women of the work party I found the tree and although the pug marks were about three days old, I could see enough to identify the killer as a youngish adult male. All four limbs appeared to be intact, yet it had taken to man eating. Why? I will explain my ideas at the end of this account.

Following a trail that is days old is a pointless and thankless task, so I returned to my camp in the Banyan grove. During the next week, two more kills took place. Although I sat up in trees overlooking the kills, the tiger did not return to its kill. I could not believe that having killed four people the tiger did not return to any of its kills. Most unusual! I could only assume that having been wounded over a kill by Mangal Thrapur, it had learnt never to return to a kill.

A couple of days later, a *shikari* was taken. He had been indulging in a little poaching and as he was approaching one of his traps he was attacked and killed by the maneater. By one of those strange quirks of fate it was the very same *shikari* who had been with Mangal Thrapur, when that gentleman was killed. It would appear that, once again, the *shikari* had displayed his customary carelessness and had paid the price. The locals suggested that he may have suffered some kind of divine retribution, whereas I favoured the careless and incompetent view. The *shikari* had been killed at about five thirty in the afternoon. By seven o'clock I was approaching the kill site. The maneater had taken the cadaver about half a mile from where the man had been killed. It had taken me about an hour of very careful tracking, in total silence, to reach the place where the maneater had consumed his meal, expecting all the time to be on the wrong end of a tiger charge. Fortunately, the situation had been helped by the local birdlife. Their reactions indicated that the tiger was not near. Even so, only a fool takes risks in that situation. About two thirds of the body had been eaten, but I knew it was pointless to hang around, as our wily maneater would not return. He had shown that his 'modus operandi' was kill, eat, move on.

The area where the kill had been eaten was largely long grass and scrub and I could clearly see the maneater's line of departure. The maneater had departed, moving off up a shallow hill. I started to follow, but progress was slow because the breeze was from in front of me and I had to zig zag up the hill to avoid giving our killer a freebie from the rear, if our assassin happened to be in the neighbourhood and saw or heard me. Eventually, the trail reached a huge bed of nettles and I could, plainly, see where the tiger had pushed through. I had no choice, I had to negotiate the nettles. Fortunately, I was wearing jungle boots and long trousers. Even so, I sustained quite a few stings on my arms, despite holding the 470 aloft, like John Wayne negotiating a swamp in a war film. Crossing the bed of nettles I found that the tiger had changed course about forty-five degrees to the left – why could the contrary animal not do that before I had to negotiate those b****y nettles! It was now starting to go downhill. It was a case of ignoring the discomfort in my arms and carry-on tracking. We soon came to an area of rocky ground that was too hard to hold a pug mark, here the trail ran out. As I was casting around, looking for any sign of the tiger, I had the strangest of feelings that I was being watched! At the same time, the hairs on the back of my neck stood on end. If I was being watched by the tiger, then it would treat me like ordinary game and stalk me into wind. Realising this, I turned to face down wind and raised the 470 to my shoulder. As I did so, a low growl emanated from a group of boulders to my front. I knelt on one knee and awaited the charge that I was convinced would come. The charge was never launched. One of my major sins – and I have a few, believe me – is that I am not very patient. Even today, over fifty years later, when fly-fishing for trout I am constantly changing the fly or trying another part of the river, so it will come as no surprise that when our killer made no move and no further sound I decided to investigate. Moving around to my right, I was keeping the rocks under careful scrutiny. I had covered a semicircle of about twenty to thirty yards and more of the rocks were becoming visible. I had almost reached the point where I expected the tiger to be waiting, when the bushes near the rock moved violently, followed by a growl.

For whatever reason, the tiger had decided that for reasons of health or perhaps it just did not want a closer look at my unprepossessing visage, it decided to run. There being no point in trying to follow, as tigers can move considerably faster than I can, I decided to head back to Vallarander. I told the *patel* where to find the body and he informed me that it would be collected in the morning. I gathered from his comments and the reaction of other villagers that the *shikari* had not been a popular or loved individual. Next morning, the body was recovered and apart from the work of a couple of jackals and a mongoose, it had not been touched. Once, again, the maneater had killed, eaten, and moved on. Further, it's reaction to me had shown that it was very aware of the damage a man with a rifle could do to its health and wellbeing.

During the next couple of weeks, the maneater killed four more people. Three men and a girl of about sixteen years of age who had been collecting water from a stream. On two occasions, a considerable number of hours had passed before I received news of the kill, as a result our killer was long gone.

In the case of the girl and one of the men, the tiger had about an hour's start on me and that with the fact that I had to move slowly when tracking was enough to ensure that our killer was gone before I found the body.

I had been pursuing this maneater for nearly a month and one Tuesday afternoon, I was having a 'bath' from a canvas bucket, inside my tent. At about two o'clock in the afternoon, a group of men arrived from a nearby hamlet and informed me that the tiger was feeding on a man, as we spoke. I didn't have time to dry and dress. I wrapped the towel around my waist, put on a pair of sandals and my hat, grabbed my 470 and a couple of rounds and set off with the men to find the body. We covered the distance to the hamlet in about twenty minutes. Following instructions from the men I began looking for the body. The kill had taken place in an area of Sal saplings and the tiger had carried the cadaver to a shallow nullah, about six feet in depth, before moving on to begin feeding. I did not make the mistake of following up the nullah – as explained in the account of the Maneater of the Babar Badans, this would have been a foolish and probably, a suicidal approach. Instead, I crept along the top of the nullah following the occasional spot of blood or a lone pug mark. As I was creeping very quietly along the bank, I noted, with some alarm and consternation, that I could hear no sound from the surrounding jungle. This meant only one thing, the maneater was close at hand! As this intelligence penetrated my dense skull, I heard a very muted growl from just ahead. So, the maneater had seen me and was displaying his displeasure at having his mealtime disturbed. Dressed as I was in towel and hat, I can only assume that the tiger had mistaken me for a native or had taken very grave exception to my 'dress code'!

The question arose of what to do next? I could hardly charge head long into dense vegetation, unless I was desperately seeking to get my beautiful, young body drastically remodelled! What to do? I noticed a few stones scattered around and picking up a couple, I threw them left-handed – a skill I had acquired fielding in the gulley, playing league cricket. As the second stone bounced into the scrub, I heard a distinct growl followed by the sounds of a heavy body departing, fast! Once, again, this very astute animal had shown a remarkable instinct for self-preservation. I knew that my chance had gone and that the maneater would not return. However, bearing in mind this animal's penchant for attacking people who had tried to hunt it, I took very great care to keep a good look out for trouble on my way back to Vallarander, as I had no desire to suffer the same fate as the late Mr Thrapur. Consequently, I was not in a very good mood as I strode through Vallarander and headed for my tent. The villagers, wisely, refrained from drawing any comparisons between my mode of dress and that of Gunga Din or Mahatma Gandhi! To be fair, just a few years later, I would have been proud of such comparisons, as I completed my university degree with a thesis on Gandhi's fasts.

One thing was certain, I was delighted that I did not have to fire the 470 with no protection for my shoulder. Firing the weapon would have hurt!

I had been hunting this killer for over a month and in that time, it had 'lifted' thirteen persons. My problem, as I saw it, was not a simple one. How on earth was I to catch up with an animal that never returned to a kill. The only factors that seemed to weigh in my favour was the fact that the killer's beat cover an area of about sixty square miles, quite a small area in reality. Secondly, the area of forest was traversed by 'Fire Lines' – tracks cut through the forest to allow for transport of logs and to prevent the spread of fire. These Fire Lines meant that I could walk around the area quite easily. Unable to think of a better plan, I decided to use these tracks and the full moon to my advantage by the simple expedient of walking the tracks in the hope of meeting the maneater. Male tigers do not share their territory with other males, so any male tiger I met was, virtually certain, to be the killer. After several uneventful night-time strolls, I set off, again, just as dark was starting to fall. I was wearing a pullover under my bush jacket and I was carrying a thermos and sandwiches in a small bag, together with my pipe and tobacco. I had been walking for about an hour along my selected Fire Line, when it was crossed by another Fire Line. In the dust of the junction, leading into the second track, I could see the pug marks of a male tiger. Pug marks are like fingerprints. No two are the same. As I looked at these pugs, I knew that I was looking at the pugs of the maneater and judging by the amount of tracks and their differing directions, the maneater was in the habit of using the Fire Line on a regular basis.

The track ran from north-west to south-east and for no particular reason I decided to head north-west. Walking slowly, I had covered about two miles, when about two hundred yards ahead I heard a male tiger calling.

Aaaaagh oooonagh, aaaaaagh oooonagh!

Hiding behind a Sal tree I gave the call of a tigress, as I had been taught by Roga, a Chenchu who had been co-opted by my mentor, David Kerr, to teach me all he could about the ways of the jungle. The effect was immediate. The tiger gave a call, indicating that he was on his way to meet his 'hot date'.

Within a minute he came into sight, growling, to indicate that he was not happy that his 'hot date' had, apparently, jilted him. He passed my tree at a range of about fifteen feet. I swivelled on my left heel, brought my rifle to my shoulder, pushed the safety catch to 'fire' and squeezed the trigger, all in one fluid movement. Daisy erupted in a shattering bang, the cordite flames dimmed my night vision, but the work was done. The bullet smashed into the tiger's skull, just behind the right ear, taking out the brains. He was dead before he hit the floor. Even so, once my night vision returned, I walked over and paid the insurance. I have seen the consequences of assuming a cat is dead, only for it to wake up and chew the unfortunate hunter to a very messy pulp.

I mentioned earlier that I would consider the strange behaviour of this tiger at an appropriate time, so here goes.

I believe that this animal was unusually bold, by nature. I say this because the normal reaction of any wounded animal is to run away and hide. They do not, as a normal behaviour, hang around in the area where they were injured, yet this one had. Secondly, it had followed Thrapur and the *shikari* to a point where it could attack and take its revenge. Again, this is not the normal behaviour of the average tiger. Unless pursued and followed, the tiger will usually run away. It will only attack when it feels cornered, even if wounded.

Next, having killed Thrapur, this very astute animal must have realised that man is the easiest animal in the jungle to hunt and kill. Why bust a gut chasing Sambhur deer or buffalo, when the hairless monkeys are so much easier to catch and kill?

Thirdly, because it had been wounded over a kill, it had learnt never to return to a kill. Thus it tended to kill more

75

people, more often, to satisfy its needs. At the same time, this behaviour was giving me no opportunity to stalk it when it was on a kill or to sit up in a *machan* and await it's return.

So, in retrospect, I think that all these factors combined to make this tiger into a maneater – only it's use of a particular Fire Line and a random choice by me, finally, lead to its demise.

In closing, let me make a point. There is a school of thought that would suggest that my ruse of using the call of a tigress and then hiding behind a tree, before shooting the tiger behind its ear, was unsporting. In my defence, I would make the case, that I was dealing with a maneater and my sole purpose for being there was to prevent further loss of human life. Had I called, whistled or coughed to attract the tiger's attention, it might have run rather than turning to fight. The result would have been more loss of life. Enough said on the subject!

Chapter 5

The Maneater of Gumballi

It was late in winter and woodcutters were busy felling trees in the forests that surrounded Gumballi. This had to be done before spring brought about a warming, that would cause the sap to rise in the trees, making them much harder to fell. A lone woodcutter was busy chopping away at a fallen log, his axe making a rhythmic sound that carried through the surrounding forests. A pantheress heard the hated sound and started to stalk the source of the hideous noise. She cleared the top of a small hill and saw the woodcutter at work. She slowed her pace and started to stalk the man, noiselessly. Descending the hill she moved around the hill, so as to keep the breeze in her face, ignoring the screams of alarm from the langur monkeys, as they followed her every move.

It did not seem to occur to her that the hated woodcutter seemed to be aware of the langurs and what the alarm calls meant. As she descended the hill, she moved around, but so did the woodcutter, always keeping his left shoulder towards the creeping cat. Slowly, she crept towards the man, using every bit of cover. Finally, when she had closed to within about fifteen yards of the woodcutter, she decided that she was close enough and she drew her hind legs underneath herself, her body trembling as she tensed her muscles for the charge that was to come. Then with a series of guttural grunts the pantheress charged. She had got into her charge, when the axe exploded and two ounces of SSG buckshot struck her in the chest, to be followed by another load of SSG. The maneater of Gumballi was dead. Walking over to her, I placed another load of the SSG underneath her left ear, obeying my golden rule, 'Always pay the insurance'. The Winchester model 12 is ideally suited to hunting large cats at close range. With the plug removed from the magazine, the pump action shotgun will take five rounds in the magazine and one in the chamber. These rounds are three-inch magnum loads, with each round carrying two ounces of pellets. In my case, I favoured the size SSG as each pellet was the same diameter as a 270-rifle bullet and it gave a load of thirty pellets per cartridge, guaranteed to distract any large cat, at a range of less than thirty yards. With the safety off, you hold the shotgun against your upper thigh and squeeze the trigger. Keeping the trigger pulled back, you work the slide of the shotgun like a trombone. As the slide goes forward the firing pin hits the next cartridge. It's possible to have ten or twelve ounces of lead airborne all at the same time and at close range it would be the height of incompetence to miss your target with that little lot! Hence my preference for using the Winchester in thick bush, when a charge might be launched from a few feet, rather than a few yards.

A few days earlier, I had been met at the nearest police station to Gumballi by Inspector Badri Sing Negri. Being the son of a policeman, I have met police officers of all shapes and sizes, but I have never met an officer with the sheer height and bulk of this gentleman, and it was all bone and muscle. Badri had been referred to me by now Chief Inspector Ramish

Gopar, of the Bangalore Constabulary. The problem that was exercising Badri's mind and, indeed, mine; was answering the question of, what had caused this animal to suddenly turn to attacking woodcutters, but without eating any of her victims. I told Badri that the whole problem did not make sense to me, as there was no logical explanation of her bizarre behaviour. Badri had asked me to accompany him to Gumballi. My task was to shoot the pantheress and his task was to try to find out why the cat had taken to killing people, but not eating them. Obviously, I would lend Badri a hand, if my expertise was of any use, in solving this fascinating problem. The first task was to question any of the survivors of these attacks. The first attack had occurred at the beginning of November, it was now near the end of December, when five woodcutters had been attacked, of these, three had been killed by the customary panther style of tearing the throat out and disembowelling. The two survivors had horrific injuries, one had claw marks all over his upper chest, whilst the second had, to all intents and purposes, suffered the removal of most of his face, such that he had to wear a mask and even his wife and children could not bear to look at him!

I do not know and, indeed, I do not want to know what methods Badri had used to interrogate the two survivors, but the man with the disfigured face decided to talk, rather than face any more interrogation! What follows is his basic account of events as related to Badri.

The five men had gone out to continue chopping wood to fulfil the contract that they had with the Forestry Department. At some point during the morning, one of the woodcutters looked under a bush to discover three panther cubs, about three weeks of age, they were probably calling for food and attracted the man's attention. In my opinion, anyone with an ounce of sense and compassion for nature would have walked away and left the cubs for their mother to return to feed. This five did not seem to possess much in the way of common sense. Instead of walking away, one of the men decided to pull the cubs out of the bush. Unfortunately one of the cubs decided to defend itself and, accordingly, scratched the man who had grabbed hold of it. Now, a three-week-old cub is not capable of inflicting any great damage, but the man who had been scratched resented his 'injury' and decided that attacking the cub with his panga – a long bladed tree cutting knife – was the appropriate course of action. Not to be outdone, the other four idiots decided to join in the 'fun'. In next to no time, the three cubs had been reduced to mangled bundles of bloody pulp! What the woodcutters did not know was that the mother of the cubs had witnessed the vicious assault on her offspring. Now, consumed with hatred and anger, she launched her attack. The first the men knew about the change in proceedings was when she landed on the chest of the first man. She fastened her teeth in the man's throat and hooked her front claws over his shoulders, at the same time she disembowelled the victim with her hind claws. In seconds, she had repeated the treatment with two more woodcutters. These three died where they fell! The two, remaining woodcutters decided that they had urgent business, elsewhere, and they set off to run. They had not gone far before the pantheress caught them, leaping on the back of one of them, she gave him a collection of scars that made him look as if his upper body had been given a going over by a berserk combine harvester. The last man made the mistake of turning to look at the assault on his friend, so the angry mum decided to rip his face off!

Having inflicted what she considered to be satisfactory chastisement she let the men go. Bleeding profusely, they made it back to the village and told anybody who would listen that they had, without any provocation whatsoever, been attacked by a homicidal cat and had been lucky to escape with their lives. Personally, I think that this account is being more than just a trifle economical with the truth! The men were taken to a nearby dispensary and thence to a hospital in a nearby town. It was some time before the men could return home.

The pantheress did not touch the bodies of the three men. Instead, she carried away the mangled bodies of her cubs, but more importantly, she took with her a pathological hatred of woodcutters. From now on, every time she heard a woodcutter, she was filled with the desire to wipe the offending cutter off the face of the earth. Like many who are filled with an all-consuming hatred, the pantheress was not thinking as clearly as she ought to have done, or she would have realised that the 'woodcutter' seemed to know exactly where she was and what she was doing. Sadly for her, she made her first and last mistake when she launched an attack on what should have been her tenth victim, me!

The manhater of Gumballi killed a total of nine people, all were woodcutters. She was not a very big pantheress, weighing perhaps eighty pounds. It is one of those appalling tragedies that need not have happened. This was the only occasion, in my hunting career, when I regretted having to shoot the grief-stricken mother of the three cubs. It may be hard to accept or believe, but even to this day, over fifty years later, I still regret the necessity of what I did!

Chapter 6

The Blind Killer of Bamundur

Head south from Bangalore, towards Ootacumund or Ooty – the so-called queen of the hill stations. Hill stations were created by the British during our benevolent rule of India. Being civil servants, the administration did not like the heat or humidity of the Indian summer, down on the plains, so they created settlements in the hills, all over India, where they could move to because of the pleasant climate. These settlements were built on hills or mountain sides; hence they were called hill stations. One of the most famous was Ooty. On arriving in Ooty, turn left and head down the Moyar valley and eventually you will arrive at the Mamundur forest bungalow, a delightful bungalow in an idyllic location, on elevated ground so that it could catch the afternoon breeze that every day blew in from the Bay of Bengal, to the east. This breeze was unbelievably cool and refreshing, especially in the heat of an Indian summer. It was in this bungalow that I stayed during my adventures with the 'Blind Killer'.

However, I am getting ahead of myself. I was attending a ball given by my employers. I was becoming very well acquainted with a young lady from the office and we were getting along like the proverbial house on fire, when there was a tap on my shoulder. Turning around, I found myself looking at the very worried countenance of Chief Inspector Ramish Gopar. Before I could say a word, Ram said, "I'd like you to come and look at a body."

As I was somewhat busy at the time, having what could only be described as very ungentlemanly ambitions towards the young lady, I don't think Ram appreciated my response of, "No thanks, I have seen plenty of bodies!" However, like all members of his calling, including my late father, who was a police inspector in England at the time, Ram was not about to be put off by my rebuttal of his request. He tried again, and again I politely declined his invitation to go cadaver viewing.

Now, Ram became more assertive. "Jock, if you do not come with me, I will arrest you." I do not know what I was to be arrested for, but I thought I had better agree rather than find out. So I made my apologies and explanations to the young lady and walked out to the Hindustan police car. Thinking that the nearest mortuary was at the Bowring Hospital, a few hundred yards away, I thought, *This shouldn't take long!* Imagine my consternation when we drove past the Bowring and I was told we were heading for the Victoria Hospital, some distance away.

We walked into the mortuary, to be greeted by a technician, who looked like a ghoul from the cast of a 'Hammer' horror film and who was standing next to a shrouded shape on a slab. Before proceedings began, Ram told me that he wanted to know if he was dealing with a murder and without further ado told the technician to uncover the body. I have every reason to believe that Ram had not seen this body before, because as he looked at the cadaver, he turned a funny ashen grey and looked as though he was inches away from festooning his evening curry all over his

83

immaculately polished shoes. He had good reason! As a result of hunting maneaters, I have seen human bodies that did not resemble a body, anymore. This corpse was in that league. It had been mangled almost beyond recognition and lumps of flesh had been ripped off indiscriminately.

Ram posed his question. "Is it murder?" I was not in a very cooperative mood, having been forced to leave a young lady at the ball where she could potentially be the victim of unsolicited approaches by unscrupulous cads! In consequence, I decided that Ram was going to pay for his indiscretions and so, when asked if the body had been murdered, I replied in the affirmative. Ram looked suitably put out by my observation and, again, asked me if it was murder. I asked Ram for a definition of murder and when he had obliged, I repeated my assertion of murder, as the victim was most certainly the subject of unlawful killing, it was definitely murder. Eventually, I think Ram must have worked out that I was playing him along, because he asked me what I thought was the cause of death.

I replied, "Death by panther." The claw marks and the fang marks around the neck of the victim confirmed me in my opinions. "Now, having sorted your problem out, I will be obliged if you will please take me back to the ball."

I returned to the ball and eventually returned to my home in Whitefields. I thought I had heard the last of this particular homicidal panther. How wrong can you be?

Next morning, I walked into the office to be met by the managing director's secretary, who informed me that my presence was required on the top floor. I was taken upstairs by the M.D'.s secretary and into his office. I knew I was in 'trouble' when I was offered a *chota peg* (a large whiskey) and a cigar that looked like a telegraph pole. As it was only nine o'clock in the morning, I accepted the cigar, but declined the alcohol. Niceties dispensed with the M.D., got down to the rat killing, as they say. I was informed that Chief Inspector Gopar had a problem and the M.D. wanted me to sort it out for Ram, quick!

Accordingly, I called around to see Ram at the local *chowki* (police station) and he gave me all the information that he had. By mid-morning, I was on my way to the Mamundur bungalow, having telegraphed the local D.F.O. to obtain permission to stay in the bungalow. This was granted and I was given the name of the *chowkidar* (caretaker) at the bungalow. Arriving at the bungalow, I settled in and had a chat with the *chowkidar*. It soon became apparent that four people had been killed by the errant panther and that all the kills had taken place in a patch of dense jungle about a mile to the north-west of the bungalow. Strange noises had been heard coming from this patch of scrub, causing the locals to ascribe the deaths to evil spirits. Whatever, this patch of scrub needed closer inspection, before doing anything else. I spent the late afternoon and evening sitting on the veranda of the bungalow going over what I knew about this strange panther.

Next morning, I set off to investigate the patch of scrub, carrying my Winchester model 12. Arriving at the scrub, I checked the wind and set off into the scrub, with the breeze on my back. Checking the game trails that ran through the brush I found that I was looking for a male panther of about average size. I spent the entire day working my way backwards and forwards through this dense brush. The only troubling problem was the occasional strange sounds that I heard. It did not make sense, as a panther, when hunting, is absolutely silent. Perhaps there was some truth to the stories about evil spirits! Also, the reactions of the local bird life such as the 'Whistling Herd boy' and the 'Brain fever bird' suggested that I was not alone in this thick scrub. Their reactions tended to indicate that there was a large cat occupying the undergrowth and with that prospect in mind I was taking every precaution against a surprise attack! I will repeat ad nauseum, that I have a very strong set of religious convictions, that I do not want my beautiful, young body undergoing a rapid transformation from the claws and fangs of a homicidal moggy! I have always liked myself, just the way I am, ugly, obnoxious, and with an evil sense of humour. If I can live with this, so can the rest of you!

I spent all day wandering round the undergrowth and I had the feeling, on occasions, that the panther was very close. However, our paths did not cross and as the sun started to descend towards the western horizon, it was time to vacate and head back to the bungalow. The *chowkidar* had prepared a lovely curry for me, for which, I was duly grateful.

Next day saw me continue my ramblings in the dense thicket of undergrowth and wait-a-bit thorns. All the time I was wandering around, I was attempting to keep the breeze on my back, as I did not want to give any anti-social local livestock, the opportunity of taking a freebie from the rear. Careless hunters do not live long, in my experience!

By mid-afternoon, I was becoming rather bored with the games and was thinking that I would go back to the bungalow, when, with no warning the local bird life told me that the panther was near. I listened carefully for any sound and thought I heard a soft rustle, like a lady's dress rubbing against furniture. I was stood on a game trail that was only a few feet wide and I was surrounded by the dense mat of vegetation. As I was looking around, I noticed that about fifteen yards ahead, the trail widened into a small glade. I started to walk towards this glade on the basis that it would give me a bit more shooting room, with less chance of me being surprised at very close range by the panther. I had just started walking, when I heard the rustling noise, again. I stopped and in a rather unnerving fashion, so did the rustling sound. You can imagine the thoughts that were going through my mind, most of these were 'Anglo Saxon' and do not bear repeating. The silence, apart from the racket from the local bird life was almost over – whelming and I do wish those b****y birds would shut up! I decided that I could turn the situation to my advantage. Afterall, the panther had no idea what my intentions were towards him, but I had every reason to believe that his intentions were very hostile. The question was 'What could I do to provoke an attack on my terms?' Then I had an idea. I ran forward the ten or so yards to the glade and turned around to face the direction I had just come from, the noise of rustling increased, and I slipped the safety off the Winchester. As I did so, a spotted body launched itself out of the undergrowth about five yards away. I fired and hit the panther in mid-air. It landed in the glade, facing away from me and I could, clearly, see the imprint on its flank where the SSG had gone home. Before it could move, I fired again, aiming at the heart, just behind the left shoulder. I, then, walked over and guess what? You are right, I paid the insurance behind its left ear. Only then did it dawn on me that after I had fired the first shot, the panther had made no attempt to run away or move, very strange indeed. When I walked round to the front of the panther, I could see the answer to my unspoken question.

The poor animal had no face. There was just a bloody mask of pulped tissue, where it's face had been. The animal was completely blind and only its jaws had survived. It had hunted its prey by using its hearing, hence the rustling noises it had made when trying to negotiate the scrub. Most animals managed to avoid it, only humans were too slow or stupid to avoid falling prey to the panther. The panther had only resorted to killing humans in order to survive, which is common with many maneaters. I took the panther to Ram and in his presence, I extracted approximately one ounce of number six bird shot from the panther's mask. I pointed out to Ram, that the shot had been fired downwards and that the wound was only a week or so old. Ram's eyes lit at this piece of information and he started an investigation, with the help of the Forestry Department and, before long, he had a name of a person who had been granted a licence to shoot birds in the forests around Bamundur. Apparently, when interviewed, the gentleman tried to deny all knowledge of events, but in the end, faced with statements from the local game rangers and a copy of the shooting permit, he admitted what he had done. He had been out shooting birds and had heard the panther calling, fearing for his safety – the panther would have avoided him at all costs – he had climbed a tree. Fate decreed that the panther walked under the tree our miscreant was hiding in and our hero had fired at the animal's head, causing the horrendous injury. This gentleman then pointed out that he was a very wealthy businessman with 'friends in high places' and that what he had done was no crime and he did not expect any repercussions or grief from a lowly chief inspector of police. Sadly for our hero, Ram did not see things in that light. Following a careful investigation and discussions with his superiors by Ram, the man was charged with some form of manslaughter, because four people had died as a result of his actions and after a trial was sentenced to some time in prison. His wealth and important friends did not save him from the ire of a very conscientious police officer!

It never ceases to amaze me how many people do stupid things without a thought of the consequences. To use an old service phrase, they 'operate with their thumbs up their bums and their brains in neutral'. In this case, four people died because of one man's stupidity. Had the man sat still and remained quiet, the panther would have continued on its way, harming no one. One of those killed had been a man called Doshi. He had been a forester and had a wife and four children. From the comments made by the locals, Doshi had been working in the scrub. He had, very obviously, not noticed the strange noises in the surrounding bush. The panther had nailed Doshi by following the sounds of work. Sadly, because of the actions of a complete moron, a woman had become a widow and four children had to grow up without a father. Heaven preserve me from idiots!

Chapter 7
The Rogue of Moyar

To those of you who have had the patience to follow my ramblings thus far, you will know that to reach the Moyar valley from Bangalore you head towards Ootacumund and then turn sharp left. Follow the road towards Moyar passing the 'Moyar Valley Ranch' built by a local entrepreneur by the name of Hughie Hailstone, in the 1930s. You eventually reach the area not far from Mamundur where the events I am about to relate took place.

Why this particular elephant became a rogue is not known. Perhaps it had been kicked out of a local herd, that had objected to his anti-social behaviour, or perhaps it had lost out in a mating tussle with another bull, but for whatever reason he had become a loner with a rather dyspeptic attitude towards the rest of the world. Whatever the reason, the animal seemed to resent every living creature that it came across and did it's best to wipe the offender off the face of the earth. It commenced its activities by catching a herd man, as he tended his herd of cattle. The rogue tore him limb from limb and then trampled the man's mortal remains into the earth. At this point, it departed for the vast wilderness of the nearby jungle. The body was eventually recovered, and the incident was ascribed to a tragic accident.

A week later, the rogue attacked a bullock cart. It smashed the cart into match wood, then gored the single bullock to death! The driver had, wisely, run away and hidden whilst all this mayhem was taking place. However, the man made the mistake of panicking and tried to make a run for it. The rogue caught the cart man and gave him a very comprehensive working over until he gave a very realistic example of death by elephant… Very messy! Within days, the rogue had struck, again. A lone traveller was caught as he walked through a dense grow of bamboo. Again, what was left of the victim would not have over-filled a couple of jam jars.

At this point, I received a letter from a Mr Rawson, the district magistrate, detailing the animal's depredations and giving me details of the animal's description and identifying characteristics. As rogues are few and far between and are, as a rule, loners; I should have no difficulty in identifying the beast. Mr Rawson closed his missive by asking me to shoot the rogue. To facilitate this end, he had enclosed a shooting permit, for the area.

Leave of absence from work, being granted, I set off for the Moyar valley. I passed the Moyar Valley Ranch and carried on for another five miles to reach my destination, the small village of Manganalli. I pitched my tent and collected water from the nearby stream. Talking to the villagers it became apparent that the rogue was rather like the 'Scarlet Pimpernel', here, there, and everywhere. Why can't rogues and maneaters be more co-operative and considerate and hang around waiting to be shot, I just do not know! As it stood, I would have to go looking for our miscreant.

Knowing that I was hunting an elephant, I loaded my 470 with blunt nosed, steel jacketed, solids, rather than my normal soft points. Afterall, the bullet would need to pass through two feet of honeycombed skull in order to reach the elephant's brain.

I spent several days hunting in the dense forest, looking for the animal. During this time, I found two elephants. One was a rather small and quite young animal that in no way matched the description of Mr Rawson's killer. The second elephant was a very elderly bull that seem to spend its days wandering through the forest from one patch of bamboo to another; judging by its great age, it was probably looking for somewhere quiet and peaceful to die. He did not fit the description, either.

Early one morning, I was approached by a small group of cart men, who informed me that one of their number had not arrived at a nearby village to collect a load. They asked me to go and look for their colleague. To this I agreed, and I set off to walk the track that the cart man should have followed. I had been walking for about an hour and a half, when I came across what looked like a largish pile of broken timber at the side of the track. A few yards further along the track I saw the carcase of a dead buffalo that had been very obviously been gored to death by an elephant. The measurements of the front feet indicated that I was looking at Mr Rawson's rogue's handiwork. Of the cart man, there was no sign. As I was studying the carnage and the multitude of tracks in an effort to determine the direction our pulverising pachyderm had taken, I heard a very faint groan coming from the wreckage of the cart. Listening carefully, I realised that the faint noise was coming from underneath the pile of broken timber. Carefully, I pulled the wreckage of the cart from the point where the noise seemed to be emanating from. Eventually, I found something that resembled a victim of an air accident. I leant over him and he groaned, again.

My problem was how to attend to, or help the man, without having to put my rifle down, leaving me defenceless against a sudden sneak attack. I, certainly, couldn't carry the man and my fourteen-pound rifle back to the nearest source of help. However, I put my rifle down by my knees, in order to examine the poor man's injuries. I gently lifted the man up, slightly, to give him a drink from my water bottle. As I did so, an unmistakable gurgling sound came from the man. As the death rattle ended, he fell silent and his chest stopped moving, as he breathed his last. Gently, I laid the body down and closed the eyes, there was nothing else I could do for the late cart man.

Feeling very chastened, I got to my feet and picking up my rifle I set off for my tent, over an hour's walk away. As I reached the village, I found the cartmen waiting for news. I told them what I had found, and I asked them to accompany me and collect the remains of their dead friend, to this, they quite readily and willingly agreed. On finding the wreckage of the cart, the pitiful remains of the late cartman, were loaded on to the bullock cart. Some time was taken because one of the cart men had been a particular friend of the deceased and he broke down at the sight of what was left of the dead man. It took some time to comfort the man, but eventually we set of and took the cadaver back to the village for cremation.

As if realising he had increased the antipathy of the locals to a new and higher degree, the rogue seemed to disappear into the vastness of the forestry block. I spent a lot of time and effort looking for the rogue. Apart from getting very hot and sweaty from the effects of the summer sun, I had little to show for my many hours of effort!

It is often the case, that when something seems to go away, the local populace begin to go about their business as they did before the problem arose. In this situation, of course, disaster struck, big time! A man, called Pari, was walking along a forest track and apart from keeping an eye open for passing carnivores, he had not a concern in the world. This tranquil state of affairs did not last. He heard the shrill trumpet of a charging elephant, goaded by fear, he started to run, but a shuffling elephant can move a lot faster than a sprinting man. Usain Bolt could probably hold his own for the first fifty yards, but the result would be inevitable and very terminal! The rogue caught Pari, it ripped his head off and threw it into the forest. It then stood on the man's chest and one at a time ripped the arms and legs off and flung them into the forest. The rogue then trampled the torso into a very messy pulp! It was becoming rather tiresome, collecting pulverised bodies, so something needed to be done!

As I sat in front of my tent, drinking tea and smoking my pipe, I thought about the situation and slowly an idea developed – contrary to popular belief, I do have the odd lucid thought. To hatch my plan I would need the help of at least one of the cart men. When I explained my plan, one of them immediately volunteered to help, not surprisingly, it was the cart man who had been most upset by the loss of his friend.

My plan involved driving slowly in a covered cart along the forest tracks, with me sitting in the back with my rifle across my knees. We headed down the track towards Segur, hoping the rogue would attack the cart, it did not, and on reaching Hughie Hailstone's Moyar Valley ranch without a hitch, we turned around and completed the reverse journey without let or hinderance as the lawyers would say. We arrived back at the village just before sunset and I had time to cook a meal before I turned in for the night. Next day, we tried the same technique, again, and we set off along the road at about ten o'clock, following the track towards the Moyar Valley ranch. We had been travelling for about an hour, when from the jungle on the right that consisted mainly of densely growing bamboo, I heard the trumpeting scream of a bull elephant. I called to the cart man to stop and jumping down, I turned to face the horrendous noise. The trumpeting was coming from a dense thicket of bamboo and I could see the tops of the bamboo waving and bending under the impact of a very heavy body. Suddenly, the bamboo in front of me parted to reveal a very large elephant, with its trunk curled up out of harm's way as is the custom with a charging elephant. I raised 'Daisy-May' to my shoulder and pushed the safety catch to the 'fire' position. The only certain shot with an elephant is the brain shot. To achieve this, you have to imagine a stick passing through the skull from one earhole to the other. No matter where you are shooting from, your aim is to break the stick in the middle, taking out the brain and dropping the elephant in its tracks.

Taking my own advice, I aimed to break the stick and squeezed the trigger that unleashed Daisy. In response to the sound of the rifle and the kick of the recoil on my shoulder, the rogue dropped on to its front knees and knelt there swaying. Noting the grey rimmed hole in the forehead, trickling blood, exactly where I had aimed for, I walked around to the side and, you guessed, didn't you? I placed the insurance round behind the left ear, again, breaking the imaginary stick. The rogue was definitely dead and proved it by collapsing towards me. In my experience, anybody when shot always collapses towards the rifleman.

Calling to see Mr Rawson on my way back to Bangalore I can state without fear of contradiction that he was a very happy district magistrate.

Chapter 8

Pachyderms, Muggers, and Snakes

The Asian elephant differs from its African cousin in a number of particulars. Firstly, it is smaller. An Asian bull stands about nine feet high at the shoulder. Only an Asian bull elephant has tusks and the head of both male and female has two distinct domes on top of the head, on either side. The back tends to be convex in shape, whereas the African elephant's back slopes down from just behind the shoulders to the tail. The skin of an Asian elephant is eighteen to twenty millimetres thick. To aid identification, it will be found that twice the circumference of the front pad will give the height of the animal at the shoulder. Asian elephants have a very good sense of smell and very acute hearing. However, their eyesight is poor and provided you are down wind and do not move, the elephant will not become aware of your presence. The following fact may surprise you, but elephants are very good swimmers and often use their trunk like a giant snorkel.

The elephant's heart is a huge organ, situated just behind the front elbow. The heart or lung shot has nothing to commend it, as the animal can travel quite a distance, when shot through these organs, before it finally drops. The only reliable shot is the brain shot. To achieve this, you must imagine a stick passing through the ear holes, from one side of the skull to the other. Using a rifle that will fire full-jacketed bullets, for maximum penetration, you aim to break the stick in the middle, no matter where you are firing from! This way you can guarantee to take the brain out, producing instant death.

By and large solitary elephants tend to be the ones to cause problems, and this is due to a number of causes. Firstly if a bull becomes too much of a nuisance for the herd to tolerate, the ladies of the herd cordially invite him to leave, by the simple expedient of pushing the bull until he leaves. Next, once a year, a bull will become sexually active, and he secretes an oily discharge from glands on his temples. This is known as the period of 'Musth' and any bull in this condition becomes very aggressive and very dangerous. Domesticated elephants are chained up to prevent problems, during this period.

If a bull has been injured in a mating tussle with another bull, they can become very vindictive and are to be avoided. As a general rule, lone elephants are dangerous and should be avoided at all costs. Herds of elephants do not cause problems, unless they have very young with them, in which case an overprotective mum can be one to avoid. One last point should be mentioned. Elephants do not like the colour white, for this reason, milestones in India are black with white lettering, rather than white with black lettering. White milestones will be ripped out of the ground and flung to the four points of the compass.

Every year, there is an elephant festival at Kandhi on the island of Sri Lanka. The largest tuskers are decked out in the most expensive and gorgeous robes and then paraded through the streets of Kandhi by torch light, lit sandal wood, not the battery powered jobs. The elephants are accompanied by hundreds of people carrying venomous snakes. Surprisingly, no one seems to get envenomated!

Finally, one piece of information for the pub quiz. Domesticated elephants are allowed to kill three mahouts (elephant jockeys) before they are put down in the interests of good work force harmony.

I had an interesting experience with an elephant, as I will now relate. On a very hot summer morning, I made my way from the bungalow in Whitefields, where I was living, to the office, in my WWII Willy's jeep. I turned the air conditioning on by the simple expedient of lowering the canvas hood and then lowering the windscreen, on the jeep. Quite cool and refreshing! After about an hour at the office, I decided that I had suffered enough in the heat and I decided to leave work and go to the Bangalore Cricket Ground and watch a game, as I had an open invitation to use a private box. As I was leaving the office car park, I found myself in the biggest traffic jam I have ever seen. I managed to wriggle into the middle of three lanes and found myself stuck behind a large cow elephant. As the law required, she had a bell on her tail to warn everybody that she was on the move. Do not laugh gentle reader, there is a good reason for this, there is an awful lot of truth to the old saw which states that the black stuff between an elephant's toenails is the remains of slow natives! Ouch! We came to a total stop. A cyclist decided to prop himself up on my off-side front wing. A bus was behind me and a taxi was on my inside. The cyclist and I were having a chat about cricket when I noticed that we had a problem. The elephant, let's call her Gertie, slowly backed up until her back legs were touching my front bumper, she then lifted her tail, complete with bell.

Then I heard an ominous rumbling noise, and I knew full bloody well what was about to happen! About five hundredweights of stinking green coconuts descended on the bonnet of my jeep. Oh Gertie, how could you behave in such an unladylike fashion? The reaction on all and sundry was amazing, pedestrians scarpered to a man! The cyclist took off pedalling like Bradley Wiggins who had suddenly remembered that he was late for an appointment in a cycle race many miles away. The taxi driver was trying to get up on the kerb whilst, at the same time, trying to prevent his breakfast from filling the footwell of his Hindustan. The bus driver, bless him, was having no luck, whatsoever, trying to reverse up in traffic and at the same time as he was producing wonderful mechanical noises from the gearbox!

Fortunately, the pile of steaming coconuts was having no effect on me, as I had absolutely no sense of smell, I still have very little after all these years. I had been cauterised up both nostrils about a year before I travelled to India. So, now people know why I could sit up over a rotting, fly-blown corpse, waiting for a maneater to return without being sick or feeling nauseous. Having lit my pipe, I noticed that a gap was appearing in front of me as people tried to get away from what I have been told is the most obnoxious, offensive, and gut-wrenching smell imaginable. I started to inch forward and in next to no time I reached the roundabout on MKG road. The policeman, on traffic duty turned a funny green colour and hastily waved me through, I assume because he was not enjoying the aroma emanating from my jeep. I chugged merrily on my way, spilling some of the coconuts as I traversed the roundabout. Eventually, I arrived home and, as was his custom, my bearer came out to greet me. Govind never displayed any surprise at any of my activities, not even when I have pitched up with a dead maneater draped across the bonnet. But I got a reaction, this day! Oh yes! Govind's left eyebrow twitched and as I said, "Can you get this sorted?" all I got was, "*Achha, Sahib*." (Yes, sir). Only after everything had been removed did we find the damage. The bonnet had a large dent in it and the paintwork had been blistered by the juices emanating from the coconuts! So, now you know why I avoid driving around the rear of any passing elephant! As a further note, I would mention that we had some brilliant roses that year.

The Mugger or Indian marsh crocodile grows to about twelve feet in length, a monster would reach fourteen feet in length. This is a lot smaller than their cousin the Nile crocodile, with whom they share the distinction of being the last surviving dinosaur. By and large, most people are safe from attack by mugger, however, there is one exception. In India, in rural areas that do not possess a village well, young girls are sent to the nearest water supply to collect water. Some of these girls are as young as seven or eight and they have to walk several miles to the nearest reservoir or tank as they are called. At one particular tank, called the Marikanave Tank, the muggers had reached epidemic proportions and they were busy taking some of the little girls, as they bent down to fill their *denchie* (a brass bowl, with a large rim.) The situation had become so problematic that the authorities had taken the unprecedented step of throwing the tank open to all forms of hunting – some of which were very unpleasant and not to be mentioned at the dining table – in an effort to get rid of the saurian menace.

I was having breakfast, when the man I shared the bungalow with, John Davis, came in and sat down. I could see that something was on his mind, I soon found out what it was. I was shown a newspaper that carried a report of the shenanigans that were taking place at Marikanave. "Jock, will you shoot a mugger for me?" It transpired that John wanted the belly skin, presumably to make a pair of shoes, because although he had many faults, I could not, in all seriousness, see John, down at the Polo Club, sporting a crocodile skin handbag! I refused to shoot a mugger and suggested that if he wanted a belly skin, he could shoot the mugger, himself. The problem was that John had absolutely no idea how to handle firearms. In the end, John cajoled me into helping him. I spent about fourteen days teaching John how to hit a target the size of a twenty-cigarette packet, at twenty yards, with my Lee-Enfield. This rifle was so accurate that most people could light a match head at the same distance, never mind hit a very large packet of cigarettes.

We set off for Marikanave, which is about one hundred and twenty miles north of Bangalore, having hired a couple of *shikari*s on the way, we set up camp near the tank. The tank is about twenty-five miles in length and about four miles wide at its broadest measurement. I took the two *shikari*s and set off to acquire a bait. I shot a Sambhur stag, and we hauled it back to the reservoir. I hauled the stag out to a sand bar, about twenty yards out, and wired it down so that the muggers could not move it. Please note the stag was about twenty yards from the bank and I had been waist deep in water when carrying out my task. I informed John that we would need to be up at daybreak. When asked what time this was, I said about four-thirty in the morning. John nearly died of shock, as he was never known to emerge from his bed before nine o'clock! I took sadistic delight in telling John that if he was not up on time, I would use a bucket of cold water as an alarm clock!

The next morning, having had breakfast, we set off for the tank. There was a thick mist hanging over the reservoir and as we crawled the last few yards to the bank edge, we could hear the wet tearing sounds of muggers, feeding. As we looked over the edge, we could see a mugger about twelve feet in length, sideways on to our position. John looked at me as though I was an alien he had seen for the very first time and was unsure what he was expected to do! I pointed just behind my ear and then pointed at the mugger. John finally got the idea and he raised my 303 Lee Enfield to his shoulder. He squeezed the trigger and as the rifle erupted, I saw the bullet lash out, cut through the mist and hit the mugger right behind the smile, taking out the brain. It was now that the fun really began. John asked me to fetch the mugger, I refused, pointing out that the mugger, undoubtedly, had equally large relatives in the reservoir that would be drawn by the scent of the blood and as you are all well aware, I have a very great interest in preserving my beautiful, young body, intact! Hence my declining his invitation to commit suicide by mugger. Next, John tried to persuade the two *shikaris* to fetch the mugger, he had as little success with them as he had had with me. In the end, it came down to the basic fact that John would have to fetch his own mugger!

Firstly, John took off his shoes and socks and then proceeded to roll up his trousers to just below the knee – why he did this is beyond me, as he had seen me up to my waist in water, the previous evening. Next, he emptied his pockets, including cigarette case, lighter and wallet and placed them on his folded jacket, then he turned to me and said, "Is your rifle loaded?" I broke 'Daisy May' open and showed him the two brass cartridges as well as the two spares between the fingers of my left hand. Satisfied that I would keep him safe, the poor, deluded, trusting soul, slowly waded into the water and waded out to the sand bar. There he stood admiring the situation and wondering what to do next. I suggested that it might be a good idea if he were to grab the mugger's tail and pull it into the water, where it would float, and he could tow the mugger back to the bank. Without further ado, John set off towing the dead saurian and had covered half the distance when events took a more sinister turn. A tremor ran down the length of the mugger and its tail move slowly sideways, before whipping back the other way. John flew through the air and landed in a thrashing pile of humanity about ten or twelve yards from the mugger, staining the water a rather peculiar shade of yellowish brown! I also noticed a strange and rather unpleasant farmyard type smell, emanating from the brown stain. Before he had hit the water, I had fired 'Daisy' and had left a crater in the mugger's head that you would need a football to fill. It was, by any standards, a very dead mugger. Losing no time, John grabbed the mugger and pulled it to the bank. Photographs were taken of the mugger with its jaws propped open to show off its dentures. John was knelt on one side of the head and one of the *shikaris* was knelt on the other side of its head. I was stood behind John.

With no warning the Mugger made a noise like a growling dog and its jaws slammed shut like a hydraulic ram. John and the *shikari* scattered. I snapped my rifle shut, thumbed the safety and put a very large hole in the mugger's neck, just behind the head. This was a very dead Mugger! We took the belly skin and departed. About four hours later, as we returned past the tank, I decided to see if the vultures had cleared the remains of the mugger, as I had been told that they could clear the remains of a large horse in less than half an hour. You can imagine my surprise when, as I approached the mugger, I could see that it was basically untouched! The vultures were all sat around in a circle, ready for dinner, with their bibs on and a knife and fork clamped under each wing, but they were not getting any closer. Then I saw the vulture that was clamped in the mugger's jaws which explained the reluctance of any other vulture to get too close. Oh boy, he had had his brain box smashed out of existence. I had parted its spinal column, we had then removed its belly skin and it had still managed to munch a vulture. I'm very glad it wasn't chasing me at the time!

Mention snakes and a lot of people get the screaming collywobbles. I must be honest and state that I do find this attitude strange, but I kept pet snakes as a schoolboy and find them quite interesting, so perhaps I am biased. To be fair, I have read that the biggest killer in India is snake bite, not car accidents as you might think. The situation may have changed in the last fifty odd years, but I doubt that very much.

With one exception, the most common poisonous snake in India, the cobra, is found around human habitation. The reason being that the cobra, along with the other snakes, feeds on mice and rats and these pests are found in corn fields or in the thatch of the village huts. Hence, cobras stay near to domestic habitation.

There are five snakes in India that can kill by envenomation. They are the Hamadryad or King Cobra, the Banded Krait, the Cobra, the Russell's Viper, and the Saw

Scaled Viper. The Hamadryad is a dark brown colour and grows to about fifteen feet in length. It is found in the jungles and feeds on other snakes. I have never met one, but the given wisdom is that they are very aggressive. The venom they inject is neurotoxic. It attacks the central nervous system, in particular the vagus nerve that controls the heart, causing heart failure. Envenomation by a Hamadryad causes death in about 90 minutes. Its fangs are about half an inch in length and the venom is trickled down grooves in the back of the fangs, so wearing thick leather boots could save your life.

The Banded Krait is, as its name suggests, a snake with bands around the body. In this case, white bands around its body. It is a small snake rarely exceeding three feet in length. It is not common and tends to live in scrub land. It is, also, a very shy snake. This snake is also neurotoxic, and a bite will produce death in about two to three hours. Its fangs are about an eighth of an inch in length and like the other neurotoxic snakes it dribbles the venom down grooves in the back of the fangs.

Next in line is the common cobra, hands up anyone who cannot describe a cobra. There are two varieties. One has what appears to be spectacles on the back of its hood, this is known as the bioccelate cobra, the cobra without the markings is known as a monocellate cobra. They are both equally poisonous, so it does not matter which one bites you! The cobra can grow up to about seven feet in length. The older the cobra, the more docile they become and providing you handle them gently they do not present a threat to your health. The same cannot be said of baby cobras. As they hatch from the egg at about six inches long, they are deadly poisonous and very aggressive, so be warned! The cobra is also a neurotoxic snake and its venom will kill in about four to six hours. Its fangs are about a quarter of an inch long and, again, they pass the poison down grooves in the back of the fangs.

The Russell's Viper grows to about five feet. It is a very stout snake and has three rows of diamond shapes down its back. Be warned, it is a very fast snake, when it strikes. This snake likes to absorb heat from the ground so is often found in open scrub or on footpaths. This makes it a dangerous snake for anyone using a path or track through scrub, at night. You may recall my apprehensions when hunting the Shirlal maneater. This snake belongs to the group known as Haemolytic snakes. The venom cause the blood to fail to clot and produces internal bleeding. Death is very painful. The fangs are about an inch in length and the venom is injected like a hypodermic, down a hole in the centre of the fang. Death occurs in about twelve to thirty-six hours. Last of the five is the Saw Scaled Viper. This snake is only found in arid desert regions. It only grows to about twenty-four inches in length and like the Russell's Viper is a haemolytic snake with fangs that act as hypodermics. Death occurs in about three to seven days.

Fact! Snakes are deaf, they have no organs of hearing, so shouting and singing will have no effect. It is not the snake charmer's tune that keeps cobras quiet, it is the rhythmic swaying of the snake charmer, who takes good care to stay just out of striking range, that keeps them safe. Snakes are very sensitive to vibration such as footfall, so you might think that stamping your feet is a good idea and so it is, unless you happen to be hunting a maneater. Remember, the big cats have incredibly sensitive hearing and if they hear your tiny tootsies they have at least two choices open to them, scarper, or creep up behind you and… Whoops!

A thought for you. According to experts who have studied snakes for many years, death from envenomation occurs in less than fifty percent of bites. However people with a weak heart can die from referral shock so you are dead, anyway. Factors that could affect snake bite mortality include how much venom is injected. If the snake has recently had a meal, it may not be able to inject much venom. The health and fitness of the victim may also help the survival chances.

In years gone by, the standard treatment for snake bite, until medical attention could be obtained was to put a ligature between the bites and the flow of blood to the heart. Then with a very sharp knife, cut across the puncture marks and suck out as much poison as possible. Poison that is swallowed, will not harm you! Finally, rub crystals of potassium permanganate into the wound, as the chemical reaction tends to neutralise some of the poison. Then find medical help.

John Davis had an interesting experience with a cobra, as I will now relate. The bungalow that we shared had four bedrooms and four bathrooms, but only one shower room, that had been built very much later. In consequence, we used to take it in turns to use the shower first, when we arrived home from the office. On this particular day it was John's turn to shower first, so I disappeared on to the veranda with a large Gin and tonic and my pipe. I had been sat there for a few minutes when John's bearer came hurtling out and said, "*Sahib*, Davis *Sahib* says bring gun to shower, *jildhi* (quickly)."

I thought, *What is going on?* After all, as you are all aware by now, John had no idea what to do with any form of firearm and he was in the shower, after all! I walked through the bungalow, grabbing a double barrelled twelve bore and a couple of number 6 cartridges from the gun room. I opened the door to the shower to be met by a truly gruesome, indeed grotesque sight. John was in the far corner of the shower, dressed only in his birthday suit, balancing on one leg whilst, at the same time covering his family jewels with both hands! Don't laugh. In the opposite corner, about eight feet away was four feet of cobra with its hood inflated. Interesting! In order to be absolutely sure, I asked John what the problem was.

He replied in a very soft whisper, "There's a snake in the shower."

Pretending not to hear him – I can be a terrible tease – I, again, asked him what the problem was. The reply was repeated, but a little louder than before.

I think my next question may have upset John and given him the impression that I was indulging in a monumental leg – pull. "John, why are you whispering? The snake is deaf, it can't hear a thing!"

"THERE'S A SNAKE IN THE B****Y SHOWER, YOU B****Y DAFT B****RD!" He yelled at the top of his voice. I pointed out that if he swore like that, again, I would leave him to it. In very placatory tones, I was beg, nay, beseeched, to deal with the snake. I loaded the shotgun and then asked John if he would care to shoot the cobra. Again, he swore indicating that he wanted me to stop messing about and deal with the situation, as well as at the same time, he was casting serious doubts on the veracity of my birth certificate. I did feel very upset and aggrieved at this suggestion that my parents had never married, being a sensitive, little soul – if you believe that, you will believe anything! Next, I explained that when I fired the gun, bird shot would bounce off the tiled walls of the shower. John was, now stood as before, but with one hand covering his prized possessions and one hand covering his eyes.

"Are you ready?"

"Yes," came the reply.

"After three?"

"OK."

"THREE!" and I squeezed the trigger. As the echo of the shot vanished, a flesh-coloured blur shot past me heading for his bedroom and as I observed John's flaccid flanks disappearing down the corridor. I, suddenly, realised what a narrow escape had occurred. Cast your mind back to the details on how to deal with snake bites. You cannot put a tourniquet on a bare derriere, and I was NOT about to suck poison from his bare nether regions! If word had ever escaped, I could have been 'Black-Balled' at the Polo club. Oh the shame! Funnily enough, after this fiasco, John always carried out a careful inspection of the shower before performing his ablutions.

Chapter 9

The Shaitan of Segur

The valley of the Segur river where this narrative is based is about forty miles south-west of Ootacumund and, so, is a good one hundred and forty miles from my home in Whitefields. The life of the *shaitan* was very well documented in the local press. If you have read the title page of this book, then you will know that *shaitan* is the Hindi word for devil. During a career spanning just over five years, his official tally of victims was one hundred and twenty-five persons. However, I know for a fact that a number of victims were not recorded against his name because people did not report the killings, or during the early part of his career people died, at a later date, from the mauling he had inflicted. Also, the area being quite remote, communication with the outside world was not good. Later in his career, once he had become adept at killing people, nobody escaped to tell the world what had happened. I spent over a year, 'off and on', hunting this very astute killer, until our first and last meeting. I mention the time period, because I do not wish to give the false impression, that every hunt meets with success. They do not! Believe me! Also, if I were to chronicle every day that I spent looking for the *shaitan*, I would bore you to distraction!

Our story begins, when a tigress gave birth to three cubs in fastness of the vast forests that covered the Segur valley. For the first two years of their lives, the tigress protected the three cubs, and she would have willingly sacrificed her life for any of them. She taught them to hunt and to kill by breaking the neck of the victim. When the cubs were about two years old and getting close to adult size, the tigress started to make life less congenial for the three, especially the *shaitan*. She realised that the mating urge was growing in her and she needed to find a new lover and if her lover came across the *shaitan*, the lover might kill him, so she drove the *shaitan* away. The *shaitan* wandered off into the jungles never to return. For the next three years he survived by hunting game in the forests, and he grew into a very large tiger. Anyone who lived in the Segur valley could tell tales of how they had heard the *shaitan*'s deep melodious call echoing through the forest glades, especially at mating time. *Aaaaaaarh Ooooooonah, Aaaaaaaarh Oooooooonah!*

However, the *shaitan* never bothered the human inhabitants of the forest or, indeed, their cattle. He was content to hunt Sambhur, Chital, or buffalo, that dwelt in the forests.

When the *shaitan* was about seven years old, events took a turn for the worse. In a small village called Doli, there lived a rather obese gentleman called Muniappa. He was the village headman or *patel*, but he was also the local poacher. The D.F.O. had made determined attempts to catch Muniappa, but Muniappa had always managed to stay one step ahead of the D.F.O. Such is life! Full of frustrations!

One evening, Muniappa decided to indulge in his favourite pastime and go into the forest to poach a deer or a wild pig. He took his single shot breech loading shotgun and a couple of cartridges loaded with bits of nail, metal nuts, and bits of brass rod. He could not afford the genuine article, so this was viewed as improvisation. Finding a salt lick, Muniappa climbed into a nearby tree, but because of his girth, he only climbed about ten feet into the branches. Darkness fell and the fat headman settled down to wait. It was a moonless night, and he could not see very far. He had been in the tree a couple of hours when he heard a wild pig snuffling in the undergrowth, waiting for the pig to emerge from the bushes, Muniappa fired his weapon. Then all hell broke loose! The pig roared, repeatedly, and the *shaitan* tore up bushes in his pain and anger. Our fat hero sat very quietly, without so much as moving a muscle. Muniappa knew that if the *shaitan* realised there was a man in the tree, his chances of living to an old age were virtually nil! Eventually, the tiger limped off into the forest, allowing Muniappa to climb down from the tree and retreat to his hut. Not surprisingly, Muniappa had a complete mental block about the events of that night and told no one of the evening at the salt lick.

Sadly, for the *shaitan*, he could not forget the events of that night. The assorted ironmongery had hit him in his left shoulder and a couple of the metal nuts had lodged in the ball joint, severely limiting the use of the left foreleg. Because of his injury, the *shaitan* was unable to kill his normal prey and as he lost weight, he was forced to hunt the rats that lived in the bamboo thickets and even they proved a challenge for him. The *shaitan*'s weight dropped to about two hundred pounds and hunger was gnawing at his stomach. In this emaciated condition, he climbed with great effort to the top of a nullah, about twelve feet high, that overlooked a game trail, hoping that something he could kill would pass along the track below. He had been laying on the edge of the nullah for over an hour, when a herd of cattle passed by and at the rear was a small calf. The *shaitan* knew he could manage to kill the calf; the problem was that a herd boy was about fifteen feet behind the calf. The boy was whistling a well-known song 'Gori, gori'. He did not have a care in the world and was paying scant attention to the cattle.

The pangs of hunger drove the *shaitan* to an act of extreme desperation. He launched himself on to the calf, breaking the neck, instantly. The boy snapped out of his daydream and realising what had happened he did a very brave, but very stupid thing. Whirling his staff around his head, he ran at the *shaitan* shouting at the top of his voice and hoping to frighten the tiger into leaving his kill. The *shaitan* was too hungry to be deprived of his meal. He spun around and with one blow of his good paw, he smashed the back of the boy's head, caving the skull in like a watermelon. The *shaitan* then ate the calf. As he rose from his kill, curiosity got the better of him and he walked over to the dead herd boy and ate part of the body near the shoulder, almost as if making a comparison. At this point in time, a maneater was born! The boy's body was recovered the following day, by a search party that had gone out to look for him.

The *shaitan*'s next kill was no accident, it was deliberate and without provocation. A *dhobi whallah* (laundry man) was leading his three donkeys loaded with washing along the path that ran from the village of Chaki to the smaller village of Doli. The *dhobi* man was passing through an area of scrub. He couldn't hear the sounds of any feeding elephants and, so, he assumed he was safe. He failed to register the hysterical screams of the Langur monkeys or the demented twittering of the parakeets that lived in the bamboo adjoining the scrub. These birds would have warned him of impending danger. Because of his ignorance, he failed to look for any problems. He did not see the malevolent yellowish green eyes that followed his every move with an unblinking stare. The *shaitan*, noiselessly slid forward and then, with the familiar coughing grunt, he launched his attack. When all hell broke loose, the donkeys ran and did not stop until they reached Doli. The *shaitan* picked up the *dhobi*'s body and disappeared into the vast forests that surrounded the Segur valley.

All credit to the villagers of Doli, when the donkeys arrived in the village, they realised that something was wrong and they followed the tracks left by the donkeys until the pool of blood on the side of the track, together with the pug marks of a very large male tiger, told their own very sad story. With the passing of time, the *shaitan* developed his beat. Every tiger develops a beat, this is a circular route, often covering scores of miles. The reason for this habit is quite simple. Being a large animal, if the tiger remained in one area it would soon have killed and eaten all the game and it would then be facing extreme hunger. To avoid this, it stays in an area for ten to fourteen days, before moving on. Eventually after a period of time, it will arrive at the point it started from. In the case of the *shaitan*, this period of time was about three months and over the next couple of years, the villagers all along his beat began to dread the *shaitan*'s three-monthly cycle of visits. The *shaitan* had begun his depredations some time before I arrived in India. He had been indulging his taste for human flesh for about four years, when I received a letter from a Mr Patel, the District Forestry Officer. The letter was brief and to the point, it set out the problem of people being 'lifted' and asked me, very politely, if I would be kind enough to shoot the *shaitan*. Easier said than done!

Knowing that the press would have kept a note of any killings I made my way to the reading room at the Tamash Bangala (Museum) in Bangalore, armed with a large-scale map of the Segur valley. I spent a couple of hours going through back copies of local newspapers and plotted all the kills, with dates, on to the map. From this information, I worked out the *shaitan*'s beat, noting with grim satisfaction, that the citizens of Doli seemed to receive more than their fair share of kills. Accordingly, I decided that Doli would be a good starting point, especially as the evidence suggested that the *shaitan* would be visiting that village in the not-too-distant future. I arrived at Doli and at the direction of the *patel*, pitched my tent in a small, overgrown, field. As usual, I had my tent surrounded by a thorn hedge, with the intention of keeping any nocturnal visitor at bay. There are records that show that maneaters do visit hunters in their tents, at night, usually leading to the demise of the hunter – and there was me thinking that the maneater was just calling round for a *chota peg* or two, as an act of social etiquette. I had, I assure you, no intentions of joining this unhappy band!

Whilst awaiting a visit from our homicidal carnivore, I spent a few futile days wandering the surrounding jungle. Returning from one of my wanderings, I was greeted by a small group of villagers, who told me that a man had been killed about seven miles away. The kill had taken place near a track. The track was motorable and, so, I set off in my jeep to find the body. The information that I had been given, eventually, allowed me to find the kill site. I started tracking the blood trail and after about an hour's careful tracking, I arrived at a large clump of bushes. Something told me I would find the body somewhere in the crud and, quite probably, the maneater as an added bonus! I checked the breeze and moved around the bushes until the breeze was blowing on my back. This meant that I would not be surprised by a sneak attack from the rear. At least, that's the theory and we all know my opinion on theory! I began to traverse the clump of shrubbery, moving very, very, slowly. After about half an hour, I came across the cadaver, part of the back, buttocks and an arm had been eaten. There was not a sound, except the buzzing of flies, that completely covered the body. The hairs on the back of my neck were stood on end and performing a tango. All this told me that the maneater was close by. I slid the safety catch of my 470 to 'fire' and carefully examined the surroundings. Every fibre in my body was telling me that the *shaitan* was very close. Just as the tension was reaching rather unpleasant levels, I heard human voices and then, I heard a heavy body moving quickly up wind. The *shaitan* had been spooked by the voices and had gone. I could hear the voices calling, so I called to them and walked out of the dense undergrowth, to meet them. In a matter of minutes they had joined me near the edge of the bushes. The group informed me that they were relatives of the deceased and they wished to take away the body for cremation. I could have lied to them and told them that I had not found the body, so that I could go back to the corpse when they had gone and climb a tree and await the return of the *shaitan*. But I believe it would have been morally indefensible to deny the body a Hindu cremation, by lying to the relatives, so I led them to the body. I spent a good fifteen minutes trying to persuade the family to let me sit up over the

117

body and take revenge for the killing of their relative. They refused, so I let them take the body. When one of the women saw the body, she commenced screaming, hysterically. I have never heard anyone scream so loudly and for such an extended period of time. It was horrendous! The body was taken back to their hamlet for cremation, to the accompaniment of the Hindu cremation chant, 'Ram nam sat hai, Satya bol gat hai.'

The next day, knowing that the *shaitan* was in the area, I set off to have a stroll along the tracks and paths of the surrounding area to Doli, to see if I could find any pug marks. During the afternoon, I followed a narrow winding path and eventually came upon a pond or small lake. As I wandered around the lake's edge, I saw a collection of pug marks of a large male tiger, having seen the *shaitan*'s pugs on previous occasions, I knew exactly what I was dealing with. The demonstrated that the *shaitan* was accustomed to using this pool as a drinking spot. As I was studying the pugs, I realised that I was surrounded by very dense vegetation that left me very vulnerable to a sneak attack. Without hesitating, I waded into the water and waded out into the middle of the lake, where I was about waist deep in water. I knew that tigers very seldom attack across water and that if this tiger tried, and I was sure it was the *shaitan*, it would be a sitting duck if it chose to attack me. I had, no sooner, reached the middle of the lake, when a tiger roared from the very spot I had just vacated. It had to be the *shaitan* and he did not sound very happy. He circled the lake, taking good care to stay out of sight, he kept the circling going for about an hour and continued this as the light faded. The roaring and grunting continued until about three in the morning, when the racket abated. As everything fell quiet, I noticed that no monkeys could be heard calling and no bird life was chattering, all this told me that the *shaitan* was still around, so in spite of my assets being well and truly frozen, as an accountant would say, I stayed put in the middle of the lake.

Dawn broke and when I could see the undergrowth, clearly, I started to wade out of the lake, noting, as I did, that the local wildlife was going about its daily business. The *shaitan* had gone, but why the evil moggy could not have gone before my family jewels had shrunk to the size of salted peanuts, I do not know! Very ungentlemanly to say the least! I got back to my tent, pulled away the thorn bush that acted as a gate into the entrance of the thorn fence, dried myself off, had breakfast and turned into make up for my lost slumbers.

As sure as the sun would rise tomorrow, it was inevitable that the *shaitan* would strike again. It did! The *shaitan* lifted a Chenchu bird trapper, as he was tending to his traps. The Chenchu are an aboriginal group of forest dwellers. The men wear a small loin cloth called a Moocha and the women wear a sari that leaves little to the imagination. They live in huts made from grass, mud, and felled branches. The huts are usually built in a bee-hive shape and a large settlement would consist of about a dozen huts, more often, only half a dozen huts. As a group, they eke out a living by hunting and, also, by selling produce they have found in the jungles such as, honey, birds' eggs and fruit. They are highly skilled trackers and extremely knowledgeable in the ways of the jungle.

The Chenchu was taken about eight miles west of Doli and word reached me early in the morning, before I had departed for my usual stroll around the forests, so I set off to walk to the Chenchu settlement. It took me about three hours to reach the Chenchu settlement. Being expert trackers, the

Chenchu had no difficulty in finding the kill. The *shaitan* had taken the body to a small clearing that was surrounded by trees of no great height. Here, it had consumed about half of the Chenchu's body. I asked the group for permission to sit up over the body. Being practical jungle folk, they realised that my plan was the best way of avenging the death of their clan member as well as, more importantly, ridding themselves of the fiend that was blighting their lives, they agreed to my request. To assist me, the little jungle men constructed a *machan*, about fifteen feet up a Banyan tree, overlooking the kill. The *machan* was a work of art and a masterpiece and was indistinguishable from the rest of the tree. I climbed the tree and settled into the *machan*. I could clearly see the corpse. By mid-afternoon, I was ready for my vigil. I had food and water for my comfort, the branches, overhead, sheltered me from the effects of the sun. My torch was fastened underneath the fore end of my rifle, so all I needed was a cooperative maneater to put in an appearance. The Chenchus had gone back to their settlement and had, presumably, barricaded themselves into their huts. I was all alone with my thoughts.

The rest of the afternoon, into the evening, passed without note and I sat listening to the bird and wildlife of my surroundings. Dusk, then darkness fell. The moon and stars illuminated the clearing with an ethereal light and as my eyes became accustomed to the light levels, I found that I could see remarkably well. The hours of darkness dragged on, but I was not worried, by the nonappearance of the striped assassin. Maneaters do not work to a clock, when feeding, so it was quite possible that the killer could return in the early hours of the morning. I noticed that the birds of the night, such as the Night Heron and the Brain Fever Bird had taken over from their cousins of the day. Sometime in the early hours, I noted with considerable interest, that the birds had stopped chattering. This could mean that the carnivore was nearby. Just as I was reasoning this out, I noticed a smallish shape – relative to the size of a tiger – was walking towards the corpse and as it stooped over the body, I realised that it was a hyena. I could not allow a hyena to desecrate the body by feeding on it, as it apparently seemed intent on doing. I had no stones or pebbles available to me, in the *machan*, and then I had an idea – yes, another one! I reached into my jacket pocket and pulled out a spare round for the 470. I flung the cartridge and had the satisfaction of seeing the missile hit the hyena on the side of the head. The hyena did not seem to enjoy being hit by a lump of brass, lead, and cordite. It let out a scream and scuttled off into the jungle, screaming loudly. The question occurred to me. Why had the bird life stopped chattering for a lowly hyena, not something they would normally do? Then I heard the answer, a low muted growl came from the eight o'clock position, to my tree. So, the tiger was there and it, now, knew that there was someone in the tree. What would it do? The jungle remained silent for about an hour, then the bird life commenced chattering, again. The tiger had gone and because of an ambitious hyena or perhaps my own stupidity and squeamishness, in that I couldn't bring myself to let the hyena feed on the dead Chenchu. I had lost the chance to shoot the maneater. No matter, it would die on another occasion, in the future. The Chenchus arrived just after dawn and I related what had happened. They looked at the tracks and even found where the tiger had been hiding behind a bush. They thanked me for preventing the hyena from feeding on their erstwhile companion. The question bothered me of 'Why did the tiger allow the hyena to approach its kill?' Its normal reaction would have been to mangle the hyena beyond recognition. I wondered if the tiger suspected a problem and had allowed the hyena to find out, as it did! Very astute, indeed!

You may recall, that the Chenchu had been killed about eight miles to the West of Doli. The next kill took place about five miles North East of Doli. Applying simple trigonometry, the distance between the two kills was about twelve miles, a distance that a tiger could comfortably cover in three to four hours. A man had been cutting firewood about a hundred yards from where he was living, in a wattle and daube hut. The man had just returned to his labours, after eating his lunch. His wife said that the first thing she and her son aged fifteen and daughter aged fourteen knew that there was a problem was when they heard the man scream, once. There was no other sound. They all thought that the man had been the unfortunate victim of an accident, perhaps he had cut himself with his axe. They ran to help and arriving at the spot where he should have been, they found a patch of blood. The boy noticed that a feint blood trail ran down to a narrow stream a few yards away. As they arrived at the stream and found where the blood trail crossed the water, they were stunned and horrified to see the pug marks of a large male tiger in the mud of the bank. Realisation dawned on the family group and they turned and ran back to their hut. Keeping close together, they set off for Doli and on arrival, told the *patel* what had happened. The *patel* was a young man who had succeeded Muniappa, when the latter had died a year earlier. He told the tragic family that a *Sahib* (me) was hunting the killer and I could be found in my tent, in the *wyran* field. I was just finishing my lunch when the group arrived. They soon

122

imparted all they knew, and I set off to find their hut. It took me about two hours to cover the five miles and when I arrived, I soon found where the man had been killed. I crossed the stream and started tracking the tiger. A drop of blood here, a bent blade of grass there, and the occasional pug mark all allowed me to follow the killer. After I had covered a couple of miles, the trail ran into a funnel of trees, about thirty yards in length. The tunnel was very dark and very claustrophobic and about five feet in diameter and I was not over keen to enter that dank place, because the killer could have launched an attack and from any direction, but I really had no choice. I checked to make sure that 'Daisy-May' was fully stoked, pushed the safety catch to 'fire' and then checked the wind. The wind seemed to be constantly changing direction, so I lit my pipe and using the smoke as a wind gauge I entered that hideous tunnel. To say I was nervous and apprehensive, would have to be the understatement of all time. Every minute sound and every shadow had to be investigated and the situation was made worse by the lack of bird song, that indicated that the tiger was nearby and was probably watching my efforts. One factor stood in my favour, maneaters do not kill wantonly. This tiger already had a kill, so if I got a little too close for comfort, the chances were that I would get a vocal warning that I was not to get any closer. What the tiger would not realise was that I would have been deliriously happy to hear its dulcet tones because then, I would have known exactly where it was hiding. Noting the direction of the smoke from my pipe I endeavoured to make sure that I was cognizant of where any likely attack would be launched from. Eventually, I got to the end of the tunnel, noting that my pipe was going out. That walk through the tunnel had been one of the worst thirty minutes of my hunting career and was not one I would care to repeat, given a choice in the matter. The blood trail grew sparser and sparser and eventually petered out. I could not follow a non-existent track. In disgust, I returned to Doli, avoiding that nightmare tunnel, as I did. Within days, it became obvious that the maneater had moved on, following his beat. Not knowing where to go next, I packed up and returned to my home in Whitefields, having told the *patel* that I would return when the *shaitan* was expected, once more. I, also, gave him money for a telegram, just in case I was needed in an emergency.

During the next six months, I visited Doli twice, but, although the *shaitan* killed a number of people during his visits, none of the victims were ever found and so I had nothing to hunt, sit up over, or stalk, so I had to be content and be patient and we all know that patience is not one of my very few virtues. By comparison, the *shaitan* acquired a reputation for cunning and ruthlessness that far outweighed reality. It was May and all the evidence pointed to the *shaitan* visiting Doli in the not-too-distant future. I packed my gear and set off for Doli, once again. On my arrival, the *patel* greeted me like a long-lost friend and assured me I could use the *wyran* field, even though it was partially ploughed. Before long, I was settled in and the boring routine began again, of walking miles of paths and tracks in the hope of meeting the *shaitan*.

I was out one day and was walking along a game trail, when in the distance, I heard a male tiger call. Was this the *shaitan*? There was only one way to find out! A tree nearby provided cover and hidden behind it, I gave the call of a male tiger. Remember, male tigers don't like each other and if two meet, then a fight will ensue, absolutely guaranteed. The effect on our other male was startling. He gave a series of roars and I could hear him crashing through the undergrowth, he was looking for the other male and, more to the point, he wanted to fight! He passed my tree and I decided to put him to the test. I coughed, gently. He stopped and spun around. I stepped out from in front of the tree and, immediately, he crouched. I thought, *he's about to charge*, so I raised my rifle to my shoulder and lined up his forehead for a prefrontal lobotomy. At this, he spun around and took off at a very great rate of knots. This tiger was definitely not the *shaitan* and I was very glad I did not have to shoot him!

Early one morning, I was talking to the *patel*, when he made a very interesting suggestion. For some reason, the villagers had come to the opinion, that the *shaitan* was in the habit of using an old, disused, and derelict temple about three miles away, on top of a low hill, as a headquarters when he was in the area. It was definitely the time for the tiger to put in his three-monthly appearance, so perhaps I had better do a spot of investigating.

Having no better idea and, certainly, not wanting to wait for another human kill to take place, I set off for the temple, just after nine o'clock, having had my breakfast, *Chota Hazri*. The temple was very dilapidated and broken down, with the walls covered in a thick growth of creepers. The centre of the temple grounds was covered in a mixture of dense under growth and creepers. The whole area of the temple was about half an acre in extent and constituted a very un-salubrious place to while away the hours.

I checked my rifle, to make sure it was loaded and then checked the breeze to determine my line of investigation. I did my utmost, to ensure that any breeze was coming from behind me – you all know why, don't you? One of the biggest problems was the dense mat of vegetation that covered the floor of the temple. Tripping was a very real hazard, and it would have been more than very embarrassing to trip and fall and then have the maneater offer to pick you up – by the scruff of the neck! Ouch! Because of the need to be careful and watch where I was placing my feet, progress was very slow. I had been working my way backwards and forwards, across the temple, when I noticed an oven shaped recess about the size of a very large dog kennel, in the wall of the temple. This needed investigation! Checking the immediate area for any signs of the tiger and with 'Daisy-May' held well back on my hip for rapid firing, I approached the recess and looked inside. The floor was very hard, so there was no sign of any pug marks, however, even with my lack of 'nose' I could still detect the aroma of cat and I am not talking about your average domestic moggy! I sat in the corner of the recess, with 'Daisy-May' pointing at the entrance and my finger down the outside of the trigger guard and my thumb resting on the safety catch. I sat in the corner for over an hour hoping the *shaitan* would put in an appearance, however, this was not to be.

Becoming rather bored – when will I ever learn, I re-commenced my search of the temple. Not one solitary pug mark did I find, but I had the very uneasy feeling that I was being watched – the hairs on the back of my neck were performing a tango, again! However, I could see nothing, but providing I kept the breeze on my back, I was relatively safe from attack. As I have said, the temple covered an area of about half an acre and I spent the whole of that very hot summer's day exploring every bit of it and fully expecting the maneater to launch an attack at any moment. By late afternoon, I had seen enough of that temple to last me a very long time and, so, before the light started to fade, I decided to leave the temple and make my way back to my camp, taking care to avoid any cover or foliage that could hide a tiger.

I pulled the thorn barrier into place, cooked and ate my dinner and settled down to a good night's sleep. I was awakened just after dawn by the *patel*, gently calling, "*Sahib, sahib.*" I rolled off my camp bed, dressed, and then pulled the thorn barrier away and joined the *patel*. "Look, *Sahib.*" I followed the *patel*'s pointing finger and observed the pug marks, in the soft soil, of a very large male tiger, just outside the thorn barrier. Following the pug marks it was rather salutary to realise that the tiger had performed three circuits of the 'boma' obviously trying to find a way in. Not being successful, the tiger had disappeared into the surrounding jungle. Backtracking, it was obvious that I had been right to take every precaution as the tiger had obviously followed me from the temple as was illustrated by the fact that some of my footprints were over laid by the pug marks of a large male tiger. The *patel* was horrified by these revelations and he begged me to sleep in the village. Only after I had spent considerable time assuring him that I was perfectly safe and had the means, my 470, to protect myself did this well-meaning gentleman calm down.

The water supply for the village was provided by a stream that was located about two hundred yards away. So concerned had the villagers become about the dangers posed by the maneater that twice a day accompanied by me and 'Daisy-May' the villagers walked to the stream, as a group, to collect all the water they needed for the day and then walk back to the village.

Two days after my visit to the temple, I received news that a man had been lifted by the maneater as he worked one of the fields near the hamlet that he lived in. I walked to the hamlet and I was given directions to find the kill. On the edge of the hamlet, I found the field where the man had been working and I could see the pug marks of the tiger in the newly ploughed field showing quite clearly the direction the *shaitan* had gone, carrying his victim. I followed the trail and after about an hour I found the growth of dense lantana where the killer had taken his victim. Under different circumstances, it would have been very educational to find out how that sagacious maneater had negotiated the dense cover, carrying its victim. There was absolutely no way that I could follow the killer as I would have been crawling on my hands and knees and would have been completely unable to defend myself in the event of an attack! I walked around the massive clump of lantana, but I could find no evidence of any movement out of that clump, by the killer. I moved back to a large teak tree and noted that I could see both sides of the lantana, so I sat at the base of the tree, with the gentle breeze blowing on to the rear of the teak tree. I must have sat there for three or four hours when I noticed that time was moving on and it would be dark anon. With this awareness, I walked back to the hamlet and locating the cattle barn, made myself comfortable for the night. The following morning, I returned to the Lantana with a group of men and as anticipated, our killer had left in the night. We collected what was left of the cadaver and I returned to my tent.

Four days after my visit to the temple, came my first and last meeting with the *shaitan*. I was seated outside my tent, smoking my pipe. It was evening and the light was just starting to faded and within the next twenty minutes it would be night. I was about to pull the thorn barrier into place when I heard a male tiger calling, about half a mile away, in the direction of the stream. It had to be the *shaitan*, because I was not aware of any other male tiger in the immediate vicinity and remember, male tigers do not share territory. I had no time to lose. I grabbed 'Daisy-May' and dropping two rounds into the breech and another two between the fingers of my left, I set off towards the stream. I had not even the time to fasten my torch to the fore end of my rifle, so I would have to manage without it.

I had just reached the stream when the maneater called again. Tigers don't, normally, call when looking for a meal. I can only assume that having become so accustomed to killing humans, the *shaitan* was using his call as a means of striking terror into the villagers and, no doubt, it worked very well to that end. By now it was becoming dark. The maneater appeared to be following the stream. I looked around for somewhere to hide and I could not afford to waste time. The stream was about fifteen feet wide, and a clump of reeds grew from my bank into the stream for a distance of about six feet. I carefully waded into the reeds and knelt down. The water was about twelve inches deep. As I cowered in the reed bed, the far from comforting thought occurred to me, that if the tiger was on the same side of the stream as myself, then the maneater would be virtually stood on top of me before I could fire. *Oh, Mummy, why do you let your idiot son do such stupid things?* As these far from pleasant thoughts penetrated my thick skull the tiger called again and hallelujah! He was on the opposite bank. As I watched, a grey shadow moved along the bank and as the maneater started to pass me, I gently raised 'Daisy-May' to my shoulder. The *shaitan* may have seen a movement or heard the faint click as I pushed the safety to 'Fire', because he stopped and crouched, facing me, with his head between his paws. I squeezed the trigger and felt the thumping recoil as over five thousand pounds of muzzle energy erupted from 'Daisy' and covered the fifteen feet between me and the killer in less than a heartbeat. The lights went out, as the muzzle flash ruined my night vision. Even as I restoked 'Daisy' from between the fingers of my left hand, I could hear that unmistakable gurgling sound, the death rattle of a dying tiger, coming from across the stream. The gurgle stopped and I fished a small torch out of the pocket of my bush jacket and as I crossed the stream, I shone the torch on the apparently sleeping form of the *shaitan*, but the pale watery blue glaze of the eyes and the rather small hole in the *shaitan*'s forehead, now trickling blood, told the truth. The *shaitan* was dead. Even so, I never broke my golden rule and I placed a round from 'May' into the back of the *shaitan*'s head.

Later, after the village had finished celebrating the death of the maneater, an event that took most of the night and left a lot of people, myself included, with a hangover, I sat in front of my tent with a small fire for warmth and smoking my pipe. I couldn't help but reflect on the stupidity of man and how events had turned a harmless and inoffensive tiger into a killer of men. A single act of stupidity cost one hundred and twenty-five lives officially, but as I mentioned earlier, I estimate that another seventy plus victims could be added to the score sheet.

When my head had recovered, I loaded my jeep and had the *shaitan* fastened to the bonnet. On the way home, I dropped the tiger's body off at the D.F.O'.s office and headed for Whitefields. The D.F.O. was very happy.

Chapter 10

The Killer from Kouthalu

Kouthalu is a village of about thirty dwellings, one hundred and thirty miles West North West of Bangalore. It sits below a West to East ridge in the Nilgiri range, at a height of about one thousand feet above sea level. The ridge, which is some thirty-five miles in length, is covered by thick forestation, mainly Sal, a few teak, and Karpal, a tree that grows to about thirty feet in height and, that, in the appropriate season is covered in red berries that the local bear population find irresistible. The village gave its name to a tigress that took to lifting the population of at least three villages that were situated about ten miles further west from Kouthalu and on top of the ridge, at an altitude of just over two thousand feet. It may seem strange to label a maneater in this way, but the villages of Godalli, Mangalli, and Segol were too insignificant to be worthy of note, so Indian bureaucrats named the killer after the nearest village of note, Kouthalu. During her career, the tigress lifted sixty-four people during a ten-month period. This would indicate that the tigress was surviving, almost exclusively on a diet of human flesh!

I had just finished hunting the Shaitan of Segur, when I received a letter from the D.F.O., of the area around Kouthalu, a Mr Parihar. The letter gave all the details of the killer, including a map that showed that our killer was operating in an area about ten miles in length by four miles wide and encompassing the villages of Godalli, Mangalli, and Segol. It concluded by asking me to hunt the animal, because the local population were living in abject terror of the killer. Having had no indication of a maneater operating in the area, I was a little surprised at the letter, until I realised that the area was so remote that reports of any kills would be very slow to reach the outside world. I wrote back, to the D.F.O. and confirmed that I would attempt to hunt the tigress. I set off the following day and covered the one hundred and thirty miles to Kouthalu. On arrival, I discovered that there was no road link to the three villages, only a footpath, and so I would have to walk to Godalli, a distance of about ten miles. Godalli is a village of some twelve huts. I set off carrying a large Bergens rucksack and 'Daisy-May'. On meeting the *patel* of Godalli, I was told that if I cared to camp in a nearby clearing, there was a small stream, nearby, that would provide me with water. The *patel* willingly agreed to have a thorn boma built around my tent. After I had pitched my tent and the boma had been constructed, the *patel* showed me around the village. Many of the doors to the huts had claw marks, where the tigress had attempted to gain entrance and the village had an aura of people living in fear and dread. The claw marks gave me an idea. There was a hay rick in the centre of the village, surrounded by the dwellings. The rick was about six feet in diameter and about fifteen feet high and I reasoned that it would make an ideal *machan*, the *patel* agreed. I felt that there was a very good chance of the maneater visiting the village and if I was sat on the hay rick, I would have a very good chance of shooting the maneater. All I needed, now, was for

133

the maneater to cooperate and pay a call on the village. Everyone was told to stay indoors and to barricade the entrance to their dwellings.

Sunset saw me climb a very primitive ladder and settle myself on the top of the rick. I pulled the straw up and around myself, as well as sticking some straw in the leather band of my hat, to help to break up my silhouette. I settled down to wait. About one thirty in the morning, I heard shouting coming from the village of Mangalli, about two miles away and I thought, *This sounds like trouble*. I was right. Almost immediately, the *patel* arrived at the foot of the rick and informed me that the noise could only mean one thing: the tigress had secured a victim in Mangalli. I got down from the rick and decided that I would walk to Mangalli. The *patel* was horrified at my suggestion, and I think my decision only confirmed what the poor man had been told about all Englishmen – mad, the whole lot of them! I explained that the tigress had just killed, and she would take the body away to eat it. On that basis, she was not likely to be near the path and if she was, she would give me a verbal warning if I got too close. Tigers did not kill wantonly, they kill when they need to eat. I felt that there was little risk of an attack, unless I made the mistake of getting too close to her kill. The moonlit night gave me reasonable vision and I wanted to be in a position to track the killer, at first light, and if I avoided any obvious ambush places, then I should be safe from attack on my way to Mangalli. I fastened my torch to the fore end of the rifle and set off. It took about an hour and a half to reach Mangalli. The path meandered through the trees and was lit by a near full moon. It was a rather ethereal and ghostly sort of a light that illuminated my way, but at least I could see where I was going. The journey had no alarms and beyond listening for sounds of the maneater feeding, all I had to concentrate on was the wind direction, which was blowing from the valley up on to the ridge, meaning any attack would come from the leeward side of the ridge. However, my stroll to Mangalli was undisturbed by any alarms.

On reaching Mangalli, I was faced with a scene of utter chaos. Some men were rushing about wielding *Pangas* (a long-bladed knife for cutting trees) or axes, the expression 'running around like headless chickens' sprang to mind. Everyone was shouting or screaming! One man, hiding in a hut doorway, was wielding a single barrel Cooey, 12 bore shotgun and he looked as though if anyone had crept up behind him and shouted 'Boo!', he would have died of fright. Others, mainly women and children were looking out of their huts from partially closed doors. Eventually, I found the *patel* and I explained to him why I was in Mangalli. I got a bit of a shock when he rounded on me and very aggressively demanded to know why I had not saved Batchi from the maneater, by shooting the brute. To say that I was taken aback by this outburst would be an understatement, but as the man was very obviously in shock, I let the comment go and did not react. A woman came forward and taking the *patel* by the arm, talked quietly to the him. I don't know what she said, but the man calmed down and then apologised for his outburst before, promptly, bursting into tears. It seemed that Batchi had been a close friend of the *patel*. When the *patel* had calmed down, he told me what had happened. It appeared that Batchi needed to answer the call of nature and he stepped out of his hut and around the corner. As he had crouched down, the tigress had killed him, because the other occupiers of the hut said they heard a sort of gasp and then silence. When Batchi had failed to return people finally plucked up courage to find out what had happened and that is when they found evidence of the kill and that was when I heard the shouting, when I was sat on the hay rick. I would gain nothing by trying to track our killer in the dark, as I would be unable to follow any blood trail, so I climbed into a cattle bier and settled down among the cattle, knowing that in the unlikely event of the tigress returning to the village, the cattle would warn me. The chances of the tigress returning were negligible, as she had a kill to feed on and would not need to approach the village.

Dawn broke, and I was offered a mug of tea and a couple of chappatis for breakfast. Next, I was shown the blood at the side of the hut. I set off to follow the blood trail, having declined the help of two men who had volunteered to help me. I declined this help for reasons I have delineated many times, in other parts of my narratives. I followed the trail as it descended across the slope of the ridge and had covered a distance of about a mile, when I came to a shallow cleft in the hillside. This cleft was about two to three feet deep and about a similar width. The blood trail had nearly petered out, but it was obvious that the killer had gone up the cleft. I started to climb the slope and, as I did so, a covey of Chuka partridge exploded from above me on the hillside and they flew off down the slope screaming their alarm call, nearly giving me heart failure in the process, I might add! As the partridge flew away, I saw a movement up the cleft and then saw the hindquarters of the tigress disappearing into the undergrowth. I did not attempt a shot, as the only one left open to me was the 'Texas brain shot'. In case you do not know, gentle reader, the 'Texas brain shot' is one that is fired up the animal's derriere, more in hope than expectation of hitting something vital! I was not prepared to risk wounding and, thereby, causing days, weeks, or months of suffering to the maneater. So I did not risk a shot. Some people will criticise me for not risking a shot, but my sole purpose in hunting maneaters was to kill, quickly, and with the minimum of suffering to the maneater. The idea of wounding a maneater, deliberately, just to give me a blood trail to follow was, and still is, abhorrent! OK, so I am a big Jessie! I will put my hand up to that one! I followed up the cleft and shortly I found what was left of Batchi. The tigress had eaten most of both legs and the chest of the deceased. I, now, had no trail to follow, so I moved back, travelling down the slope taking very great care to guard against any surprise attack. I returned to Mangalli and collected five men, including the *patel* and together, we returned to collect the mortal remains of the late Batchi. We took the remains back to the village for cremation. Batchi was the sixty-first victim of the killer.

After this sojourn in Mangalli, I returned to Godalli. Here I had a long chat with the *patel* and, as a result, I realised that the tigress would follow her usual 'beat' and that all being well, she would visit the area around Segol to look for another meal, in the next few days. Accordingly, I packed my tent and other bits and pieces and set off for Segol, a distance of about eight miles. The walk took me about three hours, not bad going with a large rucksack on my back. I was about three miles from Segol, when I met a man, carrying a large bag, heading in the same direction as myself. The man looked terrified and seemed delighted to see me. It transpired that the man was the *Tappel Wallah* (postman) and he had the unenviable task of taking the post from the post office in

Kouthalu to the three villages of Godalli, Mangalli, and Segol. His sole means of defence was a large wooden staff and a fat lot of good that would be against a maneater, so it is no surprise that he was delighted to see me and, more importantly, my rifle. We continued our journey and, now, having a companion, he told me all about the depredations of the tigress. Having arrived at Segol, I sought out the *patel* of the village. He could offer me no place to pitch my tent, but he could offer me the use of a hut about fifty yards from the village. I took him up on his offer and made several modifications to the hut, that I will not bore you with, but they made the hut tigress proof. Segol was built on the actual ridge and consisted of about fourteen dwellings and although surrounded on three sides by very dense forests, the view to the West gave a fabulous view of the Nilgiris (Nilgiri, literally means 'Blue Mountain' and is the home of the Nilgai or blue bull, a large member of the deer family).

Having settled in, my next task was to plot a means of dealing with the tigress. To do this, I needed to know the features of the area and, so, I spent a couple of days walking the paths and glades that surrounded Segol. On the second afternoon, I was walking a about a mile from the village and the path was enclosed on all sides by Karpal. This tree grows about thirty feet in height and has dense foliage that starts about six feet from the base. The base of the trees is often surrounded by dense undergrowth, often of thorns. All of this makes visibility, rather restricted. I had walked this path several times, without the slightest concern, but this afternoon, as I approached a particularly dense area of scrub, I had a very uneasy feeling that all was not right! The hairs on the back of my neck had suddenly stood on end and my hands had become a little sweaty, then, almost like pulling a switch the bird life stopped chattering and at the same time a Monal pheasant gave its alarm call and lumbered into the air from the north side of the path.

I had company!

I immediately checked the wind, it was blowing from the top of the hill, southwards, so any danger would be found on the South side of the path. One particularly dense area of vegetation attracted my attention and as I approached it, I raised my rifle to my shoulder and backed as far as possible to the other side of the path, walking very slowly and carefully, I inched my way past the foliage that was giving me concerns. I had just about cleared the danger, when a soft growl emanated from the undergrowth. I stopped and waited for the tigress to do something, I was only about six feet from the bushes, but I reckoned that was enough room to deal with any charge! I stood there for about five minutes and I saw and heard nothing, then I heard a barking deer, about fifty yards away, give its alarm call. The tigress had moved and with her had gone the danger, with a huge sense of relief I could continue to Segol. On arrival back at Segol, I told the villagers what had happened, and that the tigress was in the area and warned them that they needed to take care. That night, everyone barricaded themselves in their homes. I fastened a thorn bush across the door of my hut and bedded down for the night. Surprisingly, the tigress paid no visit to the village or my hut and I, for one, had a sound night's sleep.

Next morning, for no particular reason, I decided to remain near the village. Perhaps, I was subconsciously considering the prospect that the tigress would stay near the village and try to find a meal. Mid-afternoon, a group of three men entered the village in a hurry and in great distress. They and another man had been tending their herd of cattle in the Sal forests of the North slope of the ridge, when, with no warning the tigress had seized the missing man and had carried him off into the Sal forest. Noting that one of the men had a twelve-bore shotgun, albeit an old hammer gun, I asked him why he had not fired at the tigress. He admitted that he had been so frightened by the actions of the tigress in attacking, that he had completely forgotten to fire – I suspect that the real reason was that he was terrified of the consequences, if he had missed. I could sympathise with and understand that tigers do terrible things to a hunter's nerves.

Having been given instructions on how to find the kill, I set off. As I neared the location, I slowed up and started to check all possible hiding places. I, also, checked the wind to make sure that, as far as possible, I was tracking with the wind on my back. I found the cattle, aimlessly grazing without an apparent care in the world. Looking around, I found the spot where the man had been killed. This was indicated by a large pool of blood and I noticed with some satisfaction, that the blood had not congealed, completely, so tracking should be much easier, if the corpse was leaking blood. I started to follow the blood trail. At first the tigress followed the contours of the ridge, but after about three furlongs, she turned to go up the slope. I checked the wind and, as I did, a rather unpleasant thought occurred to me. Had she become aware of my presence and was she laying a trap for me! I reasoned that I had done nothing to betray my presence and, therefore, could proceed with caution!

The blood trail ran up the gentle slope and crossed the path that ran from Segol to Mangalli, along the ridge. Having crossed the path, the tigress continued down the slope, until she reached a large clump of rhododendron, about thirty yards in diameter. She had obviously gone into the rhododendron, leaving me with the problem of what to do? If I tried to follow her into that dense bush, I would have to crawl on my hands and knees and I would be very vulnerable to an ambush, so to minimise the risk of my getting myself radically redecorated, I decided to circle the rhododendron and see if the tigress had emerged at some point. I started to walk around the outside of the clump and had traversed about two thirds of the circumference when I found two spots of blood, on the leaves at the side of the rhododendron. I realised that the tigress had exited the clump. Yippee! I followed the blood trail, but it quickly petered out. Now, I had a problem, because the b****y cat could have gone anywhere! I was stood, trying to figure out where the tigress had gone, but there was not the feintest indication of a track or indication of which way to go. As I was stood there contemplating my navel, I heard a child's voice. The first question to pass my mind was, 'What sort of a cretin would allow a child into the jungle with a maneater loose?' The next question was, 'Where is the voice coming from?' In fact, the sounds seemed to be coming from the direction of the path. All thoughts of tracking the tigress gone from my mind, I doubled up the slope, taking care to check any cover that could hide a maneater. My peace of mind was disturbed by the fact that I had to ignore the breeze that was blowing on my back, in order to find the child before the tigress found the youngster.

As I neared the track, I could identify the direction that the voice was coming from. On reaching the track, I found a small boy of about seven or eight years of age leading a buffalo along the path in the direction of Segol. The buffalo was called 'Kalwah'. This seems to be a common name for a buffalo, in Southern India; rather like 'Eric' or 'Billy' is a common name for Hereford bulls in England. I asked the boy his name and when he had overcome his shyness in talking to the Sahib, he told me he was called Harpal. He explained that his father had told him to take the buffalo from his home in Godalli to his uncle in Segol. Yes, his father knew all about the maneater, but he had still sent a child, instead of going himself! I can think of a few choice phrases to describe that gentleman and none of them are repeatable in mixed company. We made steady progress on our journey to Segol and having delivered the buffalo, I decided to escort Harpal back to Godalli. When we got back to Godalli, I had a few well-chosen words with the *patel* and left him with the impression that if anything happened to Harpal as a result of him being sent on a suicidal journey, I would feel no inhibitions about expressing my displeasure. When you weigh thirteen stones and stand six feet tall and you are carrying a rifle, I find that people are inclined to take you at your word! The *patel* agreed with my observations and I got the impression that he did not, particularly, like the father. After talking to the *patel*, I set off for Segol. I had spent most of the day walking, even so, I had to walk quickly to make it back to Segol before nightfall. After a meal, I turned in and slept until about two o'clock in the morning, when I was awakened by the tigress roaring from about a mile away. She only called for about a minute and then fell silent. Posing the question, why?

The following morning, after breakfast (*Chota Hazri*), I decided to investigate the path to Mangalli. I had walked about a mile, when in the dust at the side of the path, I saw the pug marks of the tigress. The pug marks were heading in the general direction of Mangalli. I started to follow and as I did so, I passed a hut, set back off the path. As I was passing, a man came running out and throwing himself at me, begged me for help. The man and his wife had been locked in the small hut, all night, waiting for someone to pass. I asked the man what had happened – having a pretty good idea that the answer would not appeal to me. It transpired that about two in the morning, their fourteen-year-old daughter had gone out to answer the call of nature. I suspect that young ladies are averse to performing natures functions in the presence of their parents and so she had taken the risk of stepping outside. They had heard a muffled noise and had left the hut, to investigate, in time to see the maneater carrying off their daughter. The woman had screamed, and the man had shouted. In response, the tigress had roared, and they had both fled into the hut and had barricaded themselves in. It was the tigress roaring at the couple that I had heard during the night.

The couple pointed out the general direction they thought the killer of their daughter had taken and I set off to track the killer. The blood trail was fairly faint, but the dew-covered grass showed the route that the cat had taken. The tigress had gone down the North slope, at an angle of about forty-five degrees east. Ahead, I could see a group of very large boulders and I wondered if the killer was hiding among them. However the Chuka partridge and the 'Whistling Herd boy' were not alarmed, so I thought that the tigress was, probably, not there. Even so, I checked the wind and slowly crept up the sloping surface of the largest rock and taking my hat off, peered over the boulder. There was a small glade, but there was no sign of the tigress. However, I could clearly see where she had lain down and then got up and walked into the Sal carrying her victim. Had she seen me? No! Had she heard me? No! So, why had she moved? Then I realised that the glade was exposed to the heat of the morning sun and the tigress had moved away to find shade. Although they live in a hot country, tigers do not like heat! If ever you want to find a tiger, then find a water source or shade or both together. She had gone to seek cool shade. I reasoned that the tigress was about thirty minutes ahead of me, so I needed to make progress, if I were to catch the killer.

I climbed down from the rock and continued to follow the tigress. I entered the Sal forest and the tracks disappeared on the carpet of detritus that covered the forest floor, so I decided to follow in the same general direction, that the tigress had taken. The birdlife was still chattering and so were the langur monkeys, so the tigress was not close at hand. Ahead, I could see something waving on a bush. As I got closer, I could see it was a sari. I continued to edge forward, listening all the time to the sounds of the jungle. Walking on the sides of my feet, to limit any sound from my footsteps and being careful not to tread on any twigs, leaves, or stones I kept my eyes ahead. Suddenly, I was sure I could see a body on the ground about thirty-five yards ahead. The langurs were still chattering, so I was reasonably sure that the tigress had left the body. I inched forward and the corpse came into full view. The tigress had eaten one leg and part of the torso, it was a truly pitiful sight. However, there was enough left to entice the tigress into returning for another meal. I decided that my best course of action was to hide somewhere and await the killer's return. About thirty yards from the body was a tumbled mass of twisted and interlocked Sal roots, from several downed trees.

If I could hide in the middle of this tangle, it would suit me fine. As even if the tigress discovered my presence, I would have plenty of time to correct her table manners, before she could reach me. I examined the mass of roots and realised that I could wriggle my way into the middle – I was much slimmer in those far off, distant days. I reasoned that the tigress would approach up wind and so I would not see or hear her before she reached the kill, however I would deal with that problem as and when it arose. I had a drink from my water flask and settled down to wait. It was about noon, when I began my vigil, and it was very hot inside those roots. The body was now covered in flies and they kept up an incessant droning all afternoon and into the evening and I suspect that the aroma from the body would be most off putting, unless, like me, you have no sense of smell. About an hour from sunset, having been enclosed for nearly twelve hours, I had another drink and prepared for the imminent arrival of the tigress. Suddenly, the langurs started their alarm call and the birdlife joined in and then took off. As for me, I had maggots crawling around inside my stomach and the distinctly coppery taste of fear in my mouth. You do not worry over much when you know where a maneater is hiding, but when you cannot see or hear them, then you do tend to become rather paranoid about your own safety and wellbeing! I thought I heard a soft muffled tread, about thirty yards away, then came a growl, followed by a scream and then silence. What in the name of Tutankhamun's tummy was that? Then I realised that as the tigress was approaching her kill up wind, she had come across a wild pig and had killed it. She had then taken the pig away, presumably to eat it in peace and quiet in the vastness of the forest.

Just as dusk was descending, proper, the langurs and the birdlife resumed normal activities. The tigress had gone, but she could have gone anywhere. I could not risk an evening stroll through the jungles, however much I would have enjoyed it under differing circumstances. I picked a Sal tree and shinned up it and then pulled my rifle up on a piece of cord that I kept specially for such occasions, in my jacket pocket. I picked a union of three branches, about twenty feet off the ground, placed my rifle across my knees and spent a very uncomfortable night. At one point I became engrossed by the strange movement of the Sal tree branches, in the moonlight, then I realised that the strange movement was, in fact, the langur monkeys playing in the tree above me. At this point, I knew I was safe from any interest that the tigress might show in my beautiful, young body, because the Langurs would warn me, long before the tigress was close enough to attack me, by climbing the tree. At dawn, I climbed down, having been assured by the langurs, that the tigress was not around. I covered the body with a few branches to prevent vultures from feeding and set off for the hut by the path.

As I approached the hut, I could see several men and women talking to the couple and as I neared, the mother of the young woman saw me and guessed my news and she burst into tears. The group agreed to come back with me to collect the body. The father and mother insisted on coming with the group. We approached the kill and I gently removed the branches and at the sight of what was left of their daughter the couple broke down and sobbed all the way back to Segol village. I returned to the little hut and fell asleep, listening to the refrain of the Hindu cremation chant. I woke at about five in the evening and having eaten, sat outside the hut, smoking my pipe. As I sat there, I reflected on the fact that the girl had only been about five years younger than me and that she had her entire life in front of her when she fell victim to the maneater. Such is fate or Kismet!

For whatever reason, the tigress disappeared of the face of the earth and I decided that she would probably head for Mangalli or Godalli, so I packed my kit and headed back to Godalli and pitched my tent in the *wyran* field – a *wyran* field is one that has gone out of cultivation. As before. I desperately wanted to prevent another loss of life, but I felt that I could do nothing until she claimed another victim. Helplessness is a terrible feeling; I can assure you! Two days after my return to Godalli, the tigress struck! A group of women had gone into the forests to collect firewood. Keeping together they should have been safe, but one of the women had strayed and in walking over to a small cluster of bushes, she had presented the tigress with an opportunity that the killer did not turn down. The other women heard a scream and looked over to see their friend being carried off by the tigress and having made her kill the tigress headed into the thick Sal forest. The women fled and ran back to Godalli as fast as they could. I was talking to the *patel* and a group of men, when the women arrived, and in a few terse sentences, they told the story of what had happened. Returning to my tent, I grabbed my rifle, water flask and a couple of chapatti, as well as my pipe and tobacco, and headed towards where the woman had been killed. I found the kill site and started to follow the blood trail, noting as I did that the breeze was blowing from my right, so I was at risk of an attack from my left and possibly from my rear. I tracked the killer, slowly and carefully.

It was located about half a mile away, just below the ridge. I decided to try the stream, first. I an hour had elapsed between the killing of the woman and my arrival in the Sal forest. After about half an hour, during which time I had covered about half a mile, I came across the remains of the woman, the tigress must have very hungry because apart from the head and feet and a few gnawed rib bones the tigress had eaten everything! Langur monkeys were playing in the nearby trees, so I knew the tigress was not around. Looking around, I could find no indication of where she had gone.

As I was pondering this problem, I suddenly remembered what a doctor had told me years before. Human flesh is very salty, and, on this basis, I reasoned that our homicidal feline would, in all probability need to have a drink of water, especially in view of the amount of human flesh she had consumed. I knew from my reconnoitring of the area over the past three weeks that there were a couple of water sources, nearby. One was a stream that emerged from the ground up on the ridge and disappeared into an area of swampy mud not far from where we were. The other source of water was a pool, about twenty-five yards would start at the muddy ground and work my way up to the source, this had the added advantage of placing the wind on my back. I found the muddy ground and noted that the Langurs were unusually silent, could this mean that the tigress was drinking from the stream? I walked very slowly up the stream, keeping a very careful watch and examining any bush or clump of grass that could provide cover for our killer. Just before I reached the source of the stream, the Langurs started chattering, not in alarm, but as they were playing. I felt that the tigress was not close at hand, otherwise the Langur lookout would have been screaming the alarm at the top of his voice, but I still proceeded with caution, until I reached the spring that was the source of the stream. There had been no pug marks, so I believed that the tigress had gone to the other water source, if she had gone looking for water, at all! I set off for the pond.

It took about ten minutes to reach a distance of about one hundred yards from the pool. I slowed up and proceeded very slowly and used the Sal trees to cover my approach. As I got nearer, I was certain that I could hear something drinking from the pond. It could have been anything, a bear, Langurs, or a wild buffalo. It could also be the tigress. I checked the wind, it was blowing from the pond to me, so that whatever was drinking would not be able to smell me and would not hear me. The problem was that if the tigress was around and she decided to stalk me I could have a real problem, spotting her. Now, was not the time to think such thoughts, as I could be losing the chance to shoot the maneater. As I approached the pond, I looked between two bushes and to my delight I saw the tigress drinking from the pond. I gently raised 'Daisy-May' and lined the sights up on her neck, just behind the left ear. The tigress was sideways on to me, so I could not take my favourite brain shot. I decided on the neck shot, as being the most effective way of killing the tigress. A tiger shot through the heart can cover over a hundred yards before it drops dead and can do a lot of damage in that time and so the heart shot is not a guaranteed stopper. The idea behind the neck shot is to aim just behind the ear and about a third of the way down the neck. Five thousand pounds of muzzle energy would either break the neck, directly, or the effect of the bullet strike against the muscles of her neck, would cause the neck to break. Dead maneater! I squeezed the trigger and as 'Daisy' erupted

149

the tigress fell forward and buried her head in the pool without a sound. I stood for ten minutes and watched, in case I had to fire again, but she was obviously dead as no tigress can hold her breath for ten minutes. This was the only occasion in my career when I did not bother to pay the insurance! The woman who had been gathering wood was the tigress's sixty fourth victim. Along with a group of men we collected her body for cremation and, at the same time another group of men collected the body of the maneater. I was happy, because at least little Harpal was safe. The tigress was an old animal, her claws were bushed out and her canines, were worn, but still there. These defects may account for her taking to man eating rather than chasing game through the Sal forests. I knew from her pugs that this tigress was the maneater.

Later that day, the tigress was carried to my jeep at Kouthalu. On my way home I called on Mr Parihar and gave him the body of the maneater, I took away the thanks and kind words of one of nature's gentleman.

Chapter 11
Tracking and Hunting

I had the guidance of a Chenchu, by the name of Roga, who taught me more in a month than I could have learnt in a lifetime, left to my own devices, about tracking and the ways of the jungle. Let's start with a very basic concept. The difference between a tiger's pugs and those of a tigress. If you look at the sketch on this page, you will see that the tiger's pugs are more rounded, whereas the tigress has pugs that are more elongated and pointed. By and large, the tiger's pugs are bigger than the female. Also, the tiger's pads are closer together and have less space between them, than those of a tigress. As a tiger or tigress ages, its pugs tend to become more rutted, and the claws tend to spread and bush out more. A panther has smaller pugs, being a smaller animal, but the same premise tends to hold good about the relative size and shape of the male and female pugs. You can gauge some indication of how old the pugs are by the crispness of the outline in the soil or dust. Obviously, the crisper the outline, the more recent the passage of the cat.

Examining a kill can tell you a great deal about who did it. Tigers tend to kill by gripping the neck of the victim and twisting the neck, forcing the victim to fall over and as they fall over, they fall heavily and in doing so, break their own neck! With the exception of the large forest dwelling panther or Thendu as they are often called, a panther kills by strangulation. It grips the throat of the victim and hangs on until the victim runs out of air, or bleeds to death. Tigers are very clean feeders, so they make an entry near the vent and scoop out the entrails and drag them ten or twelve feet from the victim, before they begin to feed. Panthers by comparison simply burrow in and mix the entrails, before eating the lot! Tigers are like dogs, when they pass a bowel motion, they simply leave it exposed and walk away. The panther behaves like all other members of the cat family. Having passed a bowel motion, it scratches earth up and covers the droppings. If you find cat droppings, you can identify the culprit.

If you find a tree with striations running down it, then you have found a tiger's claw cleaning tree. The tiger uses the scratching tree to rid itself of any rotting meat and other rubbish that it has collected in its claws. The fresher the striations, the more recently has the tree been used. A panther does not bother to clean its claws, so if someone gets a mauling from a panther, the biggest risk to their health is septicaemia, caused by all the gunge that has collected in the panther's claws. I am told that before the advent of antibiotics, hunters would sooner risk a snake bite, than a mauling from a panther.

Should you decide to pick a close quarter argument with one of the big cats, you may be interested to note that a panther, unless it has turned maneater, is more likely to give you a good raking before scarpering, leaving you bleed all over the place. The tiger, by comparison is a different proposition. Once stripes have decided that he does not like you, he will finish the job, given the opportunity.

When you are hunting or tracking, you should always track into wind, because, although the cat will not scent you, it will hear you. A big cat can hear an average wristwatch at fifty yards. This is one of the reasons I tended to take my watch off, before pursuing a maneater. Although the big cats have very little sense of smell, their usual prey has very keen hearing, a well-developed sense of smell and very good eyesight and the cats treat humans as if they were similarly equipped, so they will stalk you up into wind. If you do not approach an animal into wind, the animal will hear or scent you long before you get close. If you were tracking a rogue elephant, you would adopt this approach because elephants have a very good sense of smell and very acute hearing, so unless you are planning an early funeral always track the elephant into wind.

However, the situation is rather different when dealing with a maneater. Tigers and panthers have very little sense of smell, but they have excellent vision and hearing. Bearing this in mind, you stalk maneaters with the wind blowing on to your back, because if they are stalking you, they treat you like any other animal and work on the assumption that if the breeze is blowing from them to you, you will scent them and avoid their ambush. For this reason, they will track you from up wind or they will ambush you from up wind. Knowing this, you can prepare for the eventuality of an attack. This is the reason why, when stalking the big cats, you should always be aware of the wind direction. Also, this is the reason you MUST NEVER make a sound, either by treading on a leaf or kicking a stone etc., when tracking the big cats. Take your time, do not rush! You do not want to give them any sort of a warning or give them an advantage. Remember, CARELESS HUNTERS DO NOT LIVE LONG! Especially when pursuing maneaters.

How can you discern the wind direction? Try dropping a few wisps of grass, or a small handful of dried earth or sand. You could adopt the system that I used and smoke a pipe. Any of these will act as a wind gauge for you and should prevent you being nailed from down-wind by an antisocial feline.

I keep repeating the mantra of keep the wind on your back. If you cannot do this, for whatever reason, then zig zag, across the wind. This may be slow and time consuming, the alternative is to give the maneater a freebie from behind. Not a good idea. At least if you zig zag across the wind, then you know that the danger is alternating between your left and right sides, and you can deal with this.

When you are hunting the big cats, the local wildlife will help you. Langurs do not normally shout a warning if they see a human, but they most certainly will if they see one of the big cats. Similarly, the local birdlife will alert you to the presence of a big cat, by screaming their alarm call before going very silent. What this all means is that you must listen for the sounds of the jungle, either by day or night. If the jungle goes silent, then a big cat is near at hand. Fact! The Chenchu have a saying, 'When the jungle goes quiet, sit down and wait for the jungle to start calling again. Then you can move again.' Depending on where you are, the wildlife will be varied, but all of them whether it is day or night, will warn you with their alarm calls of the danger from a big cat. Langurs occur all over India and they are the most reliable source of warning about the presence of a big cat.

Finally, if you have to do any tracking at night, then remember the following points. Elephants have red eyes, when seen at night by torchlight. The deer family have green eyes in varying shades. The bison has eyes that are blue in reflected light. By comparison, the panther's eyes are whitish red, whereas the tigers are the opposite, being reddish white. Members of the dog family reflect as white.

Chapter 12

The Pulivalam Maneater

Pulivalam is situated in the state of Tamil Nadu, about two hundred miles South, South, East of Bangalore as the crow flies, but it is a drive of about two hundred and fifty miles along some pretty horrendous roads. The village is situated down on the plains, at a height of about three hundred feet above sea level. The forests that were dotted around Pulivalam were all reachable by road, although on some of the roads you had to take great care. The accessibility of the forests was one of the reasons that the area had suffered from the depredations of the 'Car *shikari*s'.

Let me explain how these 'sportsmen' worked. Their idea of sport was to drive along the forest roads, at night, shining powerful spotlights into the jungle. When the eyes of an animal were reflected in the light, the car was stopped and without getting out of the vehicle everyone opened fire, with whatever weapons they had. When the eyes cease to reflect the light, they drove on, oblivious to the shrieks of pain and the growls of agony from the poor victim, to repeat the process elsewhere. The blood red eyes of the elephant, the bright blue eyes of the bison, the green eyes of the deer family, the whitish red of the panther, or the reddish white of the tiger's eyes meant nothing to these poachers. Young or old, it mattered not. The only thing that mattered was killing or wounding an animal they could not even identify! Now, you could be forgiven for thinking that this account is merely a dyspeptic diatribe, by a very grumpy old man on the relative social acceptability and morality of the 'Car *shikari*s'. It is not. I mention these gallant gentlemen because the 'Car *shikari*s' played a very important role in the events that I will, now, relate.

A car full of 'Car *shikari*s' was being driven along a forest track, not far from the small village of Adanur, when they saw a pair of reddish white eyes looking back at them from the jungle. Brakes were applied and the car came to a halt. As the car came to a halt, everyone grabbed a rifle and opened fire. A young tigress was the recipient of the fusillade and she bolted into the jungle with part of her lower left jaw, badly smashed. The damage to her jaw meant that the tigress was completely unable to hunt her normal prey. Later, I asked a veterinary friend about the injury, and he suggested that the tigress would have been in very great pain for the rest of her life, and she would not be able to chew properly, because of the damage to her jaw and teeth. The tigress disappeared into the jungle, but not for long. About a week after she had been wounded, by this time she was very hungry, she saw a lorry pulled up on a jungle track and she noted that the driver had got out and was looking under the bonnet. The tigress obviously associated the lorry and similar vehicles with her injury. To this end, she crept up behind the driver and then standing on her back legs, she flayed the wretched man to death with her front claws, indicating that she was unable to use her teeth. Using her teeth, the death would have been quick and relatively painless. Being flayed to death, the unfortunate lorry driver must have suffered terribly and died in very great pain, amid terrible mental anguish. Because of the damage to her jaw, the tigress was unable to carry her victim into the jungle, so she set to and, quite literally, tore huge chunks of flesh from the cadaver, using her claws. She, then swallowed the chunks of flesh, virtually without chewing.

The lorry driver's body was found next day, alongside his lorry. I was told, at the time, that even experienced police officers were sick, when they saw the body. I was shown photographs of the corpse and, believe me, it was very messy. The tigress averaged about a kill a week and when she had killed four people, all by the same method of flaying alive, authority decided that enough was enough and I received a visit from my friend, Chief Inspector Ramish Gopar, a rising star of the Bangalore Constabulary. I was sat on the veranda of my bungalow, admiring the garden, when Ram called. Govind, my bearer, showed Ram through and then disappeared. Ram related all the events as he had been given them, by the police at Pulivalam and asked me why I thought the tiger was behaving in this way. To me, the answer was obvious, her jaw had been damaged in some way – only later did anyone find out how – and she was unable to use her teeth.

I knew what question was coming next. Oh, boy did I know what was coming next! On behalf of the police of Pulivalam, I was asked the very obvious question. "Could you go down to Pulivalam and sort this mess out?"

The next morning, I set off armed with a letter from Ram, telling the local police that I was to be granted every assistance. I called at the *chowki* (police station) in Pulivalam and showed the letter to the *havildar* (Sergeant) in charge. He assured me I would have every assistance and that I would be taken to every kill. I decided for no particular reason to stay at Adanur. On arriving at Adanur, I enquired of the village *patel* if there was somewhere I could pitch my tent. He suggested that I could use a little two roomed inspection bungalow that the forestry commission used, if I didn't mind being alone at night and in the dark, about a mile from any help, bless him!

Next morning, before going for a stroll around the area, I reflected on the information I had been given. The animal was a tigress, and she was quite young – information gained from the study of her pugs. Next, she was operating within a triangular shaped area bounded by the villages of Puthur, Kannanur, and Adanur. In the middle of this area was a large tank or reservoir and the area was riddled with streams and a couple of rivers. If I was planning on locating the maneater by finding her regular drinking place, then I was scheduled for disappointment! However, the more I thought about the situation, the more I realised that the tigress was finding her victims on the forest tracks that covered the area, perhaps these tracks could be a starting point. As a result of my cogitations, I decided to walk the forest tracks and see if I could find any pug marks, these might indicate if the tigress was using the route on a regular basis. The tigress had made her last kill near the village of Kannanur, so the likelihood was that she had moved on. Prior to the kill at Kannanur, she had killed a lone cyclist, near to Puthur and on that basis, I decided that she would probably head for the area around Adanur. Walking the forest tracks, I was looking for the pug marks of a tigress. I found pug marks, but they were of two panthers and a tiger and did not match the pugs I was looking for.

I was walking a forest track, looking for any pug marks in the dust at the side of the track. I stopped to examine a set of pug marks, but immediately dismissed them as they were the pugs of a large male tiger. As I was stood there, I noticed that a patch of shrubbery, about twenty yards away, seemed to move, but there was no breeze! I continued to watch and as I did so, a massive head appeared out of the brush. The male tiger gave me a look of mild interest and after a few heart beats, he gently lowered his head and disappeared. I hadn't moved or even raised my rifle, as I could tell that the striped gentleman had no evil intentions, towards me. About a minute later, the tiger appeared out of the brush, about fifty yards down the track, looked at me and calmly walked across the track and disappeared into the forest. Proof positive of the old wisdom, that if you don't threaten them, they will not bother you! Why can't some people take that lesson on board?

Two days later and the *havildar* called to see me in the afternoon. A man walking a forest track, near Puthur had been killed and eaten. His body had been spotted by three forestry workers. The *havildar* accompanied by a constable offered to show me the kill. I climbed into my jeep and followed the police Hindustan down the road. We arrived at the point where the man had been taken, we stopped the cars and I got out, carrying 'Daisy-May'. This was killed number five. As we walked over to the body, the young constable decided that he wanted to festoon his last meal all over the ground, near the body. I grabbed him and told him to be sick round the back of my jeep, the *havildar* looked at me quizzically and I explained that I did not want the constable's meal to cover any tracks that might help me find the killer. When hunting the Blind Horror of Bamandur I had seen corpses that looked an absolute mess. This body was in that league. It did not look human anymore! The poor victim had been flayed to death and had then had chunks of flesh ripped from the body. However, I noted with grim satisfaction that there was some evidence of gnawing, using its teeth, by the tigress. I'll bet that victims in a Hammer horror film looked healthier than this poor soul! There was no wonder that the constable wanted to be sick. I had a good look around the body and eventually found a set of tracks leading off into the forest. I told the *havildar* that he could remove the cadaver and I would follow the tigress into the forest. As the *havildar* and constable departed with what was left of the victim, in the boot of the car, I set off to track the tigress. You may be wondering why I did not sit up over the body and wait for the tigress to return to her kill and then shoot her. The answer is that with most of her kills, she ate as much as possible, leaving little or no reason to return for a second meal. I had no blood trail to follow, so I had to follow by traditional tracking, following bent grass and the occasional pug or half pug in the dirt.

I had been tracking the tigress for about an hour and I noticed that the 'Brain fever' bird, the 'Whistling Herd Boy' of the cuckoo family and the jungle cocks were all chirping quietly without a care in the world and, more importantly, the langurs in the treetops were playing happily. All this meant that the tigress was nowhere nearby. To all intents and purposes, the signs left by the tigress had long since petered out, so there was no point in my pursuing a forlorn hope. I turned around and headed back to my Jeep. I drove back to the Inspection Bungalow and settled down to a meal, with the intention of turning into sleep, after that. I had just finished my meal, when the bungalow was lit up by car headlights. I walked to the door as the engine stopped and greeted the *havildar*, as he alighted from the car. My immediate thought was that the tigress had struck, again. No! The *havildar* had a different problem, in that two of his constables had gone to visit a nearby hamlet and had not returned. They had been on foot and had both been armed with the standard single shot Lee Enfield rifle. It was now dark and because of the maneater, he was worried for their safety and, please, could I go out looking for them. I agreed and set off for the hamlet, that was not connected to any track and was located in the forest. Normally, a walk through a forest at night would have been a source of great pleasure, but with a maneater on the loose, no lapse of concentration was permitted, as every patch of shade and every blade of grass capable of hiding the maneater had to be examined. Careful attention had to be given to the chattering of the bird life, as they would tell me if the maneater was in the area.

Eventually, I found the hamlet of five huts and in a loud voice asked if the two constables were there. After some minutes, two very sheepish looking individuals appeared from one of the huts. Realising that it was becoming dark and that there was a maneater on the prowl, they had, wisely, decided to stay in the hamlet until dawn. I informed the two officers that we were setting off for the inspection bungalow, forthwith. They seemed a little apprehensive at this news and one of them asked, "What if the maneater finds us?"

I am sure, by now, that you are all aware that I have an evil sense of humour and I don't think my reply did anything for the individual's peace of mind. "You can do what you like, but I will be running away just as fast as I can!" Neither of them seemed to notice that I was carrying a 470. We set off with the two constables walking in front and I took great pleasure in pointing out that because they were in front, when the tigress attacked them, I would be able to run away and leave them to their fate. In fact, being the one at the rear, I was the individual in greatest danger from the maneater. They, then, commenced shouting at the tops of their voices, so I pointed out that the tigress would be attracted by the noise and, therefore, all the racket they were making was assuredly counter-productive for their safety. Now, there was a silence that was palpable. In fact, I preferred them to be quiet so that I could listen to the denizens of the forest at night, the 'Nightjar', the 'Did you do it' bird and the 'Night Heron'. They would tell me if the tigress was anywhere in the vicinity. We arrived back at the inspection bungalow and I drove two of the most relieved men I have ever seen into Pulivalam. When the *havildar* saw the state of his two constables, he asked me what had happened, so I explained. The *havildar* laughed for about ten minutes, with tears running down his face. In private, he told me that my treatment of his officers would probably be far more effective than the 'Dressing Down' that he was going to administer to them for their stupidity!

The tigress's next kill took place on a track close to the village of Kannanur and it was with grim realisation that I noted that the tigress was sticking to her 'Modus Operandi' of taking people who were walking along the forest tracks. The victim was a middle-aged woman, who had been to Adanur, to visit her daughter and her new grandchild. She had been on her way back to Kannanur when she had been lifted by the tigress. In conveying this information, the *havildar* said he would show me where two constables were guarding the body.

We set off, with me following his Hindustan, in my jeep. On arrival at the point where the lady had been lifted, I noticed that there was no sign of the body or of any officers guarding the aforesaid body. The *havildar* must have noticed my bemused reaction, because he quickly pointed out that the body had been dragged about fifty yards into the forest, although where she had killed the woman had the usual hall marks of gallons of gore and lumps of human flesh scattered around. My immediate reaction was to ask myself the question, 'Is this another maneater, as moving the body did not fit with the tigress's approach?' However, any suspicions were soon dispelled, when we reached the body. Can you guess how I knew it was the same tigress? The tigress had dragged the body into a clump of bamboo, she had done this by gripping the body in her jaws. All of this pointed to the fact that she was starting to use her jaws for gripping, indicating that the jaw was healing, even if she was still relying on flaying alive as her primary means of killing. Also, in this instance, the tigress had left enough of the cadaver to make a second visit, a viable proposition. My problem was that there was no tree in the immediate vicinity on which to construct a *machan* and no tree that would give me a view of the kill, enclosed as it was by the bamboo thicket. The body was in a small clearing about twenty feet across and as I studied the area, a thought occurred to me and I explained my idea to the *havildar*, who thought it was a great idea. We would cut a small hole in the front of the bamboo, that I could climb through, and then about two feet further back, a slightly larger space in which I could sit!

The *havildar* disappeared and came back about twenty minutes later, with three forestry workers. In the meantime, I had collected a rug from my Jeep and my bag, containing food, water, pipe and tobacco. The three foresters busied themselves and in no time at all my hide had been constructed. I laid the rug in the hide and using some of the cut stems, constructed a plank for me to crawl down, into my refuge. Fortunately, the bamboo was so closely grown and interwoven, that there was little risk of any of them slipping down to hit me or impale me. Once I was ensconced, the *havildar* and his merry men departed, leaving me to watch the body. It was about three in the afternoon and as it was autumn, it would be dark at about seven in the evening. I made sure that 'Daisy-May' was fully stoked and that the torch was securely fastened to the fore end and settled down to listen and watch. I had a perfect view of the body, about fifteen feet away. Hidden as it was by the bamboo, the body could not be seen by vultures or passing crows, which was a relief. About half an hour after the *havildar's* departure, the residents of the jungle resumed their normal social discourse. I was delighted, as they would warn me, long before my own sense of hearing, of the proximity of the maneater. Dusk started to fall, and the tigress should be thinking of returning to her kill. I was very relaxed, but alert. The tigress could only approach me through the small hole in front of me and 'Daisy-May' would give her a prefrontal lobotomy, long before I was in danger.

Darkness fell and I sat waiting for my eyesight to adjust to the low light levels. As my sight did so, I could clearly define the outline of the cadaver. At about eight o'clock, the denizens of the jungle became very quiet, a fact that did not go unnoticed by me! The tigress was in the vicinity. Then about twenty yards behind me I heard a noise that I will not try to describe, but I knew that the tigress was answering the call of nature. This was a good sign, as it meant that the tigress was not suspicious or concerned in any way. Hours of practice ensured that I had sat from three o'clock, without moving or fidgeting in any way, yet after half an hour, the tigress had not approached the kill. Why? Then I realised what the problem was! I hadn't realised, until I looked now, but the foresters had moved the body a few feet to one side, presumably thinking it would give me an easier shot. The tigress had noticed this move and she knew that dead bodies do not move of their own volition. Something had moved it and the tigress had developed a very itchy feeling about the body! I sat for another fifteen minutes and then I heard a gentle sigh from the edge of the clearing at about nine o'clock from my position, outside my field of fire. It was the tigress acknowledging the fact that her kill was now off limits. About half an hour later, the birds of the night recommenced their calling. I knew that the maneater had gone.

The fifty yards of jungle between me and my Jeep was very dense and not suitable for a stroll to collect my motor, in the pitch black of a jungle night. As you must all be aware, I haven't survived to my present stage of great age, senile decay, and antiquity by having scant disregard for the well-being of my beautiful, young body! I decided to sit tight. I didn't think that the tigress had become aware of my presence, so there was a remote chance that she might change her mind and return to the kill. As dawn broke, I climbed out of my hide and had a good look around. There was no indication that the tigress was anywhere at hand, so I collected my things together and headed for my jeep. The *havildar* returned, just after dawn was breaking, with three constables and a lorry with three foresters in the back. I told the *havildar* what had happened and the fact that moving the body had not been a smart move. The three foresters looked very sheepish, but not half as sheepish as they did when the *havildar* had finished with them. And I thought rugby players could swear! The body was loaded into the truck and taken to the lady's family in Kannanur. I climbed into my jeep and set off for the inspection bungalow and a good sleep.

Next day, I set off to walk along the forest tracks to see if I could spot any signs of the tigress, but the only pugs I saw belonged to my affable friend from earlier in the week. By the end of the day I had walked a good many miles. The activities of the maneater had gone very quiet and nearly a week had passed since her last kill. It could not last! It didn't! Word came to me via the *havildar*, who was called Anik, advising me of a kill near Puthur. Following our usual system, I followed the *havildar* to the village of Puthur. Here, the *patel* told us that a group of boys had been herding a flock of goats along a track, about two miles from the village, when the tigress had leapt out from a clump of bushes and grabbed a boy of about fifteen and carried him off into the jungle. The boys, when interviewed, confirmed that they could hear repeated screams, coming from the jungle and that the volume of the screams remained constant, until they stopped all together. All this indicated, to me, that the tigress had been killing the boy and because of the time scale involved, she was flaying the boy alive, but the fact that she had carried the boy from the path did indicate that she had some use, at least, from her injured jaw.

The boys showed me which path they had been following and gave me a rough indication of where the attack had taken place. Armed with this information, I set off to find the kill site, having sent the boys back to the village with the *havildar* and a constable for company. Eventually, I found the marks on the track that indicated where the boy had been lifted. There was a faint blood trail leading into the jungle. I set off to follow in the tracks of the killer. The jungle was not particularly dense, at this point, and so tracking was relatively easy. Apart from a few mild undulations, the ground was flat and by looking well ahead, I could see the trail left by the tigress, on the long grass of the jungle floor. The odd blood spot reinforced my observations. I had tracked the tigress for about a hundred yards, when I came upon the spot where the tigress had killed the boy. I hunted eleven maneaters during my career, but I have never seen anything like the sight that greeted me, nor would I wish to see such a sight, ever again. I am not squeamish, by any stretch of the imagination, but the sight that greeted me, made me feel distinctly nauseous. An area about four yards in diameter was saturated with blood and the ground was covered in lumps of human flesh, falling where they had been ripped off by the maneater. It was by any stretch of the imagination, a truly ghastly sight. There was no sign of a body, but there was a blood trail, leading further into the jungle. I noted that I could hear no wildlife, indicating that the tigress was not too far away. I started to follow very carefully, paying all due attention to the surrounding foliage and, most importantly, the wind direction that was blowing from just behind my right elbow. This meant that any attack would come from my left, or in front of me. I was pleased, because shooting from the right shoulder, I would not have to move my rifle very far if the tigress decided to spring an ambush.

The tigress had a good hour's start on me, but I could not afford to get careless or to rush after her. I had followed the tigress for about half a mile, when I came to an area of low growing conifers and shrubs. I had started to walk through this vegetation, when I noticed a slight movement from a conifer bush. I stopped and watched the conifer for a couple of minutes, at about ten yards to my right, at an angle of about forty-five degrees, a slight movement of the low growing conifers was causing me concern. Fact! For no reason I can think of, I decided to almost lay down and look under the bush. As I did so, I found myself looking straight into the countenance of the tigress, from a range of about ten yards. I knew she was the killer, because I could see the deformed lower jaw. I hurriedly raised my rifle and bedded it into my shoulder, but before I could even move the safety catch, let alone squeeze the trigger, the killer was gone! Like all maneaters of my experience, she knew that some humans are to be avoided and to this end, she disappeared into the thick undergrowth and all I could do was to listen to her very rapid departure. As I looked, again, I could see what was left of a body. I inched forward, convinced that the tigress was nowhere near, a point reinforced by the local wildlife. The body was that of the young man and the tigress had eaten most of the torso and both legs. There was no chance of her returning to her kill! I walked back to Puthur and found the Anik waiting for me. I told him what had happened, and I said that I would provide an escort for any group that went to recover the body. The *havildar* said he would accompany me and he rounded up another half dozen 'volunteers', announcing, "Don't worry, Jock, I will find some help." What is it about policemen, the world over, that they can always

169

find 'volunteers' for any unpleasant task? I warned everyone that what they were about to witness was not a pretty sight. We found the body and a couple of volunteers were 'promptly sick!' The body was collected and returned to the boy's father, for cremation.

The maneater's next kill took place along the banks of the large tank or reservoir in the middle of the area. A Water Board workman was lifted as he walked back to his truck, having delivered a load of lumber for some work. Sadly, nobody reported this killing to either my *havildar* friend, Anik, or to myself. The first we knew of events was when somebody asked, out of idle curiosity, if the killer of the Water Board man had been shot. Anik was not impressed, and I do believe he had strong words with the supervisor about a lack of cooperation and information, but there is no point 'crying over spilt milk'. The maneater's ninth and final kill took place near to Kannanur. Despite of all the warnings, people still wandered the forest tracks, alone. It was as if they thought that nothing could happen to them! The lone traveller was lifted by the maneater, about midday. Fortunately, a group of forestry workers who were nearby, heard her killing the man and they ran to Kannanur to report to the *patel*. He, in turn despatched runners to the *chowki* in Pulivalam, to report to the *havildar*.

The first I knew of developments, was when Anik pulled up outside the Inspection Bungalow and greeted me with, "The maneater has just killed another traveller near Kannanur, Jock." We drove to Kannanur in our usual formation and having spoken to the forestry workers, I set off for the scene of the attack, followed by Anik in his Hindustan. Anik said that he would like to accompany me when I tracked the killer, but when I explained that I always hunted alone and my reasons for doing so, he said he would wait by the vehicles. I suggested that I would be happier if he sat inside his Hindustan, with the windows closed, making it virtually impossible for any passing maneater to get to him and add him to the score sheet. Anik agreed to my suggestions and having made sure of his safety, I set off to track the killer.

I followed the trail, a bent blade of grass here, a pug mark there, and the odd blood spot. I had followed the tigress for about three hundred yards. After about a hundred yards, I passed the spot where she had killed the man. As with previous kills, this was not a pretty sight, as blood and flesh were scattered about. She had taken the body on, indicating that more and more use was returning to her jaw and she was prepared to carry her victims, even if she was still killing by flaying. I found the corpse and noted that in common with many maneaters, she had taken her kill into the thickest scrub she could find. I noticed that the birdlife was very quiet, but a Langur watchman was busy screaming his head off! I looked up and saw that he was looking in my general direction. Langurs don't normally scream their alarm call at the sight of a human being, but they certainly do when they see a tiger. The tiger was, obviously, very close. I checked the wind and noticed that it had moved around and was now coming from, slightly behind and to my left. Any attack would come from my right-hand side. I held 'Daisy-May' back on my hip and slid the safety catch to the 'Fire' position. It was as well that I did and had heeded the warnings of the Langur. The tigress appeared out of the scrub, to my right and more or less, exactly, where I thought she would appear from. She roared and came forward; I squeezed the trigger and 'Daisy' erupted with a shattering explosion of cordite. An ounce and a half of nickel jacketed lead hit the tigress at the point where her neck met her body. She actually seemed to take a step backwards under the impact, before collapsing with the customary gurgling sound of the 'death-rattle'. I walked forward and place the insurance round into the back of her head. You should all know by now, never let them get up for a second bite. As I examined her, I noted the horrendous damage done to her lower jaw and I couldn't help but marvel at how she had survived after the damage caused by the 'Car *shikaris*'. As I was examining her, Anik, came galloping up with his single shot 303 Lee Enfield at the ready. He had heard the growl and my two shots and had arrived post-haste, to see if I needed any help-very kind and considerate of a brave man!

His first words on seeing me were, "Jock, is that the maneater?" I showed him the damaged jaw. There was no need for any further comment.

I took the tigress to the D.F.O. and showed him the damage to her jaw. The D.F.O. had the tigress skinned and I noted with satisfaction, that my first bullet had entered the chest and as it expanded it had taken out the heart and lungs. The bullet was extracted, about twelve inches short of the tail root, a chilling testimony to the destructive fire power of the 470! In closing, I would mention that even today, there are those who travel the forests tracks of India at night, in mechanised vehicles, shooting at anything that moves. When will these people ever learn?

Those responsible for the creation of the maneater were discovered by accident. One of their number had gone to his local club and having consumed more alcohol than was good for him, he started bragging, with great hilarity, about what he and his friends had done. Unfortunately for him, one of his audience was a retired senior police officer and, in consequence, my friend Ram received a tip off. Because they had a game licence, in the eyes of the law they had been hunting and had committed no offence. However, I found out from a source, that Ram had hinted to the gentleman that if ever Jock Wilkinson needed a bait for a maneater, Ram knew exactly where to find one. I'm told that all hilarity ceased at that point!

Chapter 13
The Rogue of Ranigar

When you go to bed on a night, I assume that you, fully intend to get a good night's sleep, undisturbed by external factors other than somebody snoring. Sadly, for the inhabitants of the little hamlet of Ranigar in the foothills of the western ghats, not to be confused with a village of the same name in the Corbett National Park in the Kumaon district of northern India. Events over fifty years ago meant that sleep was not something to contemplate. A rogue elephant had taken to visiting the hamlet, at night, and inflicting considerable damage on the infrastructure of the hamlet – it flattened the huts. This pachyderm had also killed four residents, by the simple expedient of trampling and stamping them into a messy pulp, as they lay crouching in their huts, terrified by the noise and carnage taking place outside their dwellings! The outside world got to know of the elephant and its favourite pastime, when the D.F.O. reported the problem to his superiors. The superiors, in turn, contacted my managing director and, as a result, I found myself being called to the top floor, for a briefing. I was given all the latest on the elephant and its antisocial behaviour and told to go and stop the animal before any more damage was done. Let's be clear from the outset. I do not like hunting elephants. I find them very easy

174

to hunt and even easier to kill, providing you follow my maxim and 'Break the Stick, using a sufficiently powerful rifle and solid bullets'. I also find elephants very interesting, very intelligent, and by and large good-natured beasts – except when defecating on the bonnet of my Jeep – that bother no one if they are left alone. Sadly, the human race can leave nothing alone, to live in peace, hence the problems that occur from time to time, in all guises, including rogue elephants and maneaters. Having been briefed by my boss early in the day, I arrived at Ranigar just after lunch. To be fair, you could have done less damage to the place if you had driven a bulldozer through it! Three huts had been completely flattened with two victims in one hut and one each in the other two. Under the circumstances, how more people had not been killed, I do not know.

I could see, clearly, the line of departure of our pulverising pachyderm and I set off to follow, having first measure the footprints and done a drawing of them, to aid identification. Afterall, it was bad enough that I would have to shoot an elephant, but to shoot the wrong one would, in my eyes, constitute a serious crime against nature. Following the trail was easy, because unlike the big cats, the elephant cannot walk along a route without leaving evidence of its passing, in the form of very large footprints, damage to grass and vegetation, and their droppings. In the case of their droppings, a few comments are necessary. Freshly deposited elephant dung, this means less than an hour old, will be warm to the touch, have evidence of moisture in the droppings, and very obviously they will smell. As the droppings become older, the aroma tends to disappear, the moisture tends to dry up, and they develop a crust. Old elephant droppings have a markedly

175

pronounced crust and it will take some force to push a finger into them. Freshly deposited dung is very easy to penetrate with a finger – but don't forget to wash your finger before your next meal! I suspect that you will only make that mistake, once.

Having considered the biological factors pertaining to the tracking of an elephant, let us proceed. The trail led away into the jungle and I followed, listening for the sounds of an elephant feeding. This meant the sound of branches being broken off trees, or as you get closer, the rumblings of the elephant's stomach. Elephants make a noise, that is very similar to the digestive sound, but is made in the trunk and according to experts, is a sound used by elephants in order to communicate in dense vegetation. Either way, the elephant is very close, and you really should be sure that you want to find an elephant at such close quarters, before you proceed any further. It is very important to be aware of the wind direction when hunting an elephant because they have very sensitive hearing and an equally well-developed sense of smell. For these two reasons, you want the breeze to be blowing from the elephant to you, not the other way round, because that would mean that the elephant would scent you or hear you long before you get near. As I was tracking the rogue, I came to an area of jungle scrub that had been flattened. This was the work of a small herd and, unfortunately, it provided our rogue with the opportunity to mingle its footprints with those of the herd, making tracking a virtual impossibility. I walked around the perimeter of the trampled grass, hoping to find a footprint that matched the measurement and drawings I had made. Eventually, I found what I believed to be the tracks of the rogue and I set off to follow the beast. The animal was proceeding at a steady pace and I reckoned that it would take me about two hours to catch up.

I followed the tracks down to a small river and noticed that the tracks continued along the bank, rather than crossing over to the other side. As I continued on, I heard the sounds of an elephant having a bath. I checked the wind and found that the breeze was blowing towards me. I moved closer, taking care not to make any sound and eventually I found the elephant. However, unless the reports that I had been given were wrong, then this elephant was not the rogue, because this elephant was female and I had been assured by the inhabitants of the hamlet, that their molester was definitely a male, with two shortish tusks. Since finding the area of trampled grass, I had wasted over two hours chasing the wrong elephant. I left the lady to her afternoon bath. Let's be fair, ladies. You would not like a rather ugly individual, armed with a double-barrelled express rifle, coming along to interrupt your afternoon bathing ritual, now, would you? All I could do was return to the hamlet and await developments. I arrived back at Ranigar in the late afternoon and was offered dinner in the form of a very hot– oh boy, I do enjoy a very hot curry – vegetable curry. I decided that I would spend the night sat in my jeep, with 'Daisy-May' across my knees. I had been sat in my jeep, all night, with the occasional sip of water from my water bottle and the odd pipeful of tobacco, when just before dawn, I heard the sounds of a heavy body smashing its way through undergrowth. First light was just beginning to light up the surroundings. I got out of the Jeep and stood facing the direction of the noise. The noise grew louder and louder and was now accompanied by the trumpeting screams of a bull elephant. A largish elephant appeared out of the undergrowth and, as it did so, it curled its trunk up out of the way, as elephants are prone to do when they mean business. I noted the two shortish tusks and decided that I had to put an end to the frivolities. I raised my rifle, lined up the sights to break the stick and pushed the safety catch forward. I squeezed the trigger and 'Daisy' erupted. The elephant seemed to sit back on its haunches, as five thousand pounds of muzzle energy hit the elephant in the forehead. The rogue crashed to the floor and I walked around and stuck a round from 'May' into the hollow behind his ear, again, breaking the stick.

I noted that the stomach of the elephant appeared to be a little enlarged and there was a distinct smell of alcohol, coming from the open mouth. I asked the *patel* of the hamlet to open the elephant's body. This was done and as soon as we did, there was the distinct smell of alcohol, coming from the stomach. The stomach was opened, and we found the cause of the problem. The stomach was full of fermenting fruit and all the alcohol, produced by the fermenting fruit had reduced the elephant to a drunken, belligerent slob. I am told that most animals, when they get drunk, become good natured and affable idiots. Not so the elephant. Like a good number of humans, when the elephant becomes drunk, it becomes an offensive and antagonistic lout that simply wants to fight! At least we had discovered the reason for the rogue becoming an engine of destruction! It had spent it's time in the banana plantations munching the fruit and as the fruit fermented, the elephant had become totally inebriated, with consequences that we know about. I headed back to Bangalore after the fastest hunt of my career! My managing director was over the moon and thanked me for my efforts. And, no, I did not get a pay rise!

Chapter 14

The Marauder of Mysore

The Marauder of Mysore was a tiger that took it upon itself to try to decimate the population of the small village of Yadathittu and its neighbouring villages and hamlets. Mysore is the major city of the area and is about ninety miles west, south, west of Bangalore. Yadathittu is situated about ten miles north of Mysore, in the foothills of the Chamundi Hills, themselves being a foot note to the Western Ghats, that run from the southern tip of India on the west coast, northward up past Bombay, or Mumbai, as it is known today. Yadathittu is located at a height of about two and a half thousand feet above sea level and at the time I am writing about, was surrounded by thick forests of mixed deciduous trees. The area was very popular for forestry work and provided employment for a good number of the local inhabitants. Others in the area were employed in cattle and goat rearing. Yet, others found employment in Mysore, about ten miles away.

A largish male tiger of about seven or eight years of age moved down from the Nilgiri on the slopes of the Western Ghats and took up residence near the village of Yadathittu. Here, the tiger chose to feed upon the wildlife of the surrounding area, supplementing his diet with the occasional cow or buffalo. In fairness to the locals, they tolerated the tiger's activities because he did not become greedy and only took the occasional cow or buffalo. The tiger chose to demonstrate a studied indifference and good-natured tolerance to any of the inhabitants that he came across and the locals showed a very sensible attitude, by avoiding the tiger, especially if he was on his kill. However, the inevitable happened, somebody chose to operate 'with their thumb up their bum and their brain in neutral'. One of the local cattle herders, a young man of about twenty-two, whose name was Chirag, was out in the jungle, when he came across the tiger eating its kill and instead of backing off and going away, for whatever reason, he decided that he could scare the tiger away and then take the virtually complete carcase of a Sambhur stag, for his own use. Accordingly, he lit a firecracker, that he carried when cattle minding, and threw it at the tiger and followed this up with a few well directed stones. The tiger decided that he did not like the reception he had been given and he left his kill, snarling in resentment. Let it be said that providing you do not approach a feeding tiger, or a tigress with cubs, or two mating tigers, then a tiger is a remarkably affable animal that will avoid any confrontation with the human race. However, this tiger was very resentful of being driven off his kill and, no doubt, was determined that it would not happen again!

The young man was inclined to take a single barrel shotgun into the forests and indulge in a spot of poaching, shooting the occasional pheasant or Chuka partridge. As luck would have it, about a month after his confrontation with the tiger, the young man happened to come upon the tiger who, again, was feeding on a kill. Not having any firecrackers to hand, Chirag decided to fire his shotgun and, very foolishly, he aimed at the tiger. The bird shot hit the tiger on the flank, but at a range of about fifty yards did no great damage to the tiger, apart from the sting of the impact and the indignity of being peppered with dust shot. However, if the tiger was peeved by someone trying to scare him off his kill, having been peppered with dust shot he was now fighting mad! In less time than it takes to describe, he covered the fifty or so yards and seized the young man by the chest. Chirag was dead before he hit the floor. Justice having been served, in his eyes, the tiger returned to his kill, finished his meal and then disappeared into the surrounding forests. The body of the young man was untouched, until it was found by a search party and taken back to Yadathittu for cremation.

It's a pure guess, but I suspect that the tiger resented his treatment at the hands of Chirag and decided that payback time had arrived. More and more cattle were taken by the tiger and the poor people of the village could ill afford the losses. Salvation for the village came in the form of a local Indian landowner or Nawab, or at least that was the initial perception. After the tiger's next kill, the kill was located and a *machan* – a tree platform from which to shoot dangerous game – was constructed and the local Nawab was invited to occupy the *machan*! The Nawab climbed into the *machan*, armed with a 308 Winchester. This would stop the tiger, but as with all weapons, you have to hit something vital in order to have any effect. The tiger, having no cause to behave differently, returned to his kill in the evening, whilst it was still light. As the tiger approached its kill, the Nawab fired and hit the tiger, why he did not let the tiger settle to its kill and present himself with an easier shot, I do not know – later it was discovered that the bullet had passed through the tiger's stomach and out again, leaving an exit wound, about the size of a clenched fist, that became infested with maggots. The tiger disappeared into the surrounding forests and, no doubt, spent a time nursing what must have been a very painful wound! With the disappearance of the tiger, everyone thanked the Nawab for his timely intervention. With the shooting of the tiger, everything was quiet. The cattlemen returned to the forest and grazed their cattle as they had always done. In fairness to the Nawab, he did report the incident to the local D.F.O., but because the tiger appeared to have vanished, it was widely assumed that the animal was dead and the Nawab was hailed as a hero!

About four weeks after the tiger had been shot, a forestry worker disappeared from near a hamlet about seven miles from Yadathittu. Most people assumed that he had taken 'French Leave' and assumed that he would appear in due time. Perhaps no one would have taken any notice of the absence, but a week later, another forestry worker disappeared, only this man was not alone. He was accompanied by three others and these three reported that the man who was killed had become slightly separated from the other three, when he had been killed and carried off by a tiger. It was noted that the tiger appeared to have a suppurating wound on its left flank. I wonder if any of our readers could care to identify this animal? After this kill, the tiger appeared to vanish, however, he soon reappeared near the village of Hongahalli, where he lifted a woman who had gone into the jungle to chop firewood. When she did not return by teatime, her husband organised a search party. I gather that the gentleman was more concerned with the fact that his evening meal was not ready, rather than any genuine concern for his wife's welfare. The search party knew where the woman had been proposing to work and so the search party headed to that point. On arrival, they soon found her hand axe and next to it a smear of blood, the obvious conclusion being drawn that the woman had been injured in an accident and had become disorientated, so they followed the feint blood trail. About a hundred yards away, under a bush, they found what was left of the body, with clear evidence that the woman had been killed by a tiger. The search party grabbed what was left of the woman and headed back to Hongahalli, apparently, the group had great difficulty keeping up with the late victim's husband – why does that not surprise me?

The next kill took place near to the largish village of Balamuri. A charcoal burner was collecting brush to convert into charcoal, he was working his way through the brush, picking up suitable twigs, when he was lifted by the maneater. His body was found next day, both legs and a large portion of his torso had been eaten. Those who had examined the pug marks near the kills could detect no infirmity or handicap that might suggest why this animal had become a maneater. Over the next six months, the maneater lifted another thirteen people, indicating that it was not surviving, solely, on human victims. When the maneater had lifted a total of seventeen victims, I received a letter from the district magistrate, giving me full details of the animal's activities and asking me to hunt down and shoot the offending cat. Why authority has to wait until the killer had racked up seventeen kills, I do not know. It is far easier to hunt a maneater before it becomes too experienced and wily. I sent a telegram to the D.M., accepting his commission and I set off for Yadathittu, as all the information I had been given suggested that as the tiger followed it's 'beat' it was due to visit the area around Yadathittu in the not-too-distant future.

The road from Bangalore to Mysore being a good one, I covered the distance to Yadathittu in about three hours, arriving just before midday. I introduced myself to the *patel*, to find that he had, already, been advised by the D.M., to expect my arrival. The *patel* offered me a choice of three different camp sites and I chose one that was about fifty yards from the village and had a small stream about thirty yards away that would provide me with water. Once my tent was erected, I had the usual thorn enclose put around it, to discourage late night visitors. The area around Yadathittu could best be described as open parkland, in that it had the usual growth of mature trees of various species, each about twenty to thirty yards apart. The trees being interspersed with bushes and shrubs. It was an area that any tiger would be happy to occupy, as the territory provided ideal cover for a big carnivore, without the scrub being too dense to make movement difficult. Members of the deer family found the area congenial, so the big cats had meals on the hoof, readily available. Because of the open nature of the parkland, the locals favoured it for grazing their cattle. Everybody was happy.

Everyone in the village and, indeed, the surrounding hamlets, was well aware that they could expect a visit from the 'Mysore Maneater' at any time in the not-too-distant future. When people went out to go about their business, they did so in groups of half a dozen in number, or more. Even the cattle herders stuck together for safety. However, it was the cattle herders that suffered, next. A group of them, numbering five, were sat near a bush having their midday meal. They should have been safe from attack, but they were not. The maneater, suddenly, appeared around the bush and grabbed the nearest man, as it was killing the man, the other men ran off as quickly as was possible. They were about two miles from Yadathittu, but they covered the distance in no time. I was having lunch, outside my tent when the *patel* brought the men to see me.

Having been given all the details, including how to find the kill, I set off, having declined the help of one of the herders, to show me the kill – we all know why, by now, don't we? When I arrived within about half a mile of the kill, I slowed up and checked the wind. A gentle breeze was blowing from my right and slightly in front at what I would describe as the two o'clock position. Using the large trees as cover and being very careful to check every piece of scrub, I inched forward. When I reached a distance of about two hundred yards from the kill, I could hear the feint sounds of the tiger feeding. I moved forward, the sounds of feeding growing louder and louder. I noticed that I could hear a couple of crows, calling and eventually, I located them in a tree overlooking the kill. They were looking at the maneater, presumably waiting for the killer to move off, so that they could feed on the remains. I continued to inch forward and could see part of the tiger's outline, but the scrub was covering the vital areas, so I decided to inch forward to get a better shot. As I moved forward, I noticed that the crows were, now, watching me and the tiger, in turn, by swivelling their heads from side to side. All I needed was for the crows to concentrate on the maneater and let me get close to my target. I was now about thirty yards from the killer, when the crows let out a loud cawing and took to their wings. As they took off, the sounds of feeding came to an abrupt end. Now, I could be in trouble. I edged closer to the kill and could see no sign of the maneater and it's when you can't see them that you need to worry! I approached the kill, taking very great care to examine every bit of cover to make sure I did not get any unpleasant surprise. The Kill was partially under a piece of scrub, as I bent down to examine the body, I could feel the hairs on the back of my neck stand on end. My sixth sense was telling me that the tiger was close at hand. I checked the breeze and found that it was, still, coming from my two o'clock position, so any attack would come from my left. I lifted my rifle up on to my hip and as I did so, I heard a grunt from the brush on my left and I had a glimpse of a tiger's body departing, rapidly. Once again, that sixth sense that maneaters seem to possess had warned it that the man it was stalking was very hazardous to its health. I walked around the brush and as I did so, I could see the feint impression of the tiger's pugs in the leaf litter of the forest floor. I started to follow the trail. I had been following the tracks for about an hour when I approached a pile of rocks ahead of me.

I had a feeling that the rocks could be hiding the maneater, so as I approached, I slowed right up and slipped the safety of my rifle to the 'fire' position. I very slowly inched my way past the rocks and as I did so, the tiger growled from the biggest group of rocks, but the tone of the growl was different, it indicated to me that the maneater was not enjoying the process of being pursued by someone who was not put off by the growls. There was a definite tone of fear in the tiger's reaction. As I checked the area for signs of the maneater, it became obvious that the tiger had done a runner. Eventually, I found signs of the tiger's departure and started to follow.

Unfortunately, after about an hour, all signs had disappeared and in a landscape that was relatively flat and featureless, I could not even guess the direction that the killer had taken. In consequence, I had to give up and return to Yadathittu. Here, I collected a group of men and we returned to collect the mortal remains of the late herdsman. I noticed, as we collected the body parts, that some of the body was, apparently, missing and I was of the opinion that the maneater had returned to feed on its kill, after I had departed to fetch a cremation party. All this indicated to me, that the killer was nearby. I called the men together and told them that they must keep together and walk in front of me, because I was convinced that the tiger was close by. As we were about to set off, we all heard a low growl, coming from about forty yards away, in the direction in which I had tracked the animal some four hours earlier. We set off, walking slowly, with me walking at the rear and in greatest danger from attack by the maneater, if it should choose to launch one. After we had covered about a mile, I became convinced that the maneater had given up and had departed for other regions, because the local birdlife was chattering, and Langur monkeys could be heard calling in play. Soon we arrived back at Yadathittu and in next to no time, the cremation of the remains was taking place.

The maneater's nineteenth and last kill took place in the early afternoon, a few days later, near a small hamlet that was not far from the village of Hongahalli. I was out walking in the opposite direction, as it happened, looking for any signs of the maneater. A search party was organised to find me and eventually, they did. They knew that they were safe looking for me, as the kill was in the opposite direction and their chances of meeting the maneater were, virtually, nil. Their news was imparted, and we set off, as a group, to find the corpse. The group said that they would come with me, as they felt safer walking in front of me and my rifle. We arrived at the kill and I studied the area. A more awkward place could not have been imagined. The tiger had found a large clump of grass, about twenty or thirty yards across, in the middle of an area about two hundred yards across that was totally devoid of trees, or bushes. The body had been deposited alongside the clump of grass and I had no doubt that the maneater would approach its kill through the cover of the waist high grass, to make sure that it was not seen. I had no tree to build a *machan* on, in fact the only place where I could sit was in the grass. My problem was that I could not watch in all directions for the approach of the cat. Common sense suggested that if I chose to sit in the grass, I should do so with my back to the cadaver. Further, I had the devil's own job, persuading the relatives of the dead man to let me use the body as bait. Eventually, the *patel* came to my rescue and pointed out that if they wanted retribution for the death of their loved one, then they had to let me sit up over the body. Finally, they agreed. Now, I had the unenviable task of sitting in the grass and awaiting the return of the maneater. At this point, the *patel*, again, came to my rescue. He suggested that we sit back-to-back in the clump of grass and if the maneater approached from his side, a nudge in the back would be the signal for me to take action.

I was not happy with this idea, but the *patel*, called Dipak, asked me how many maneaters I had shot and when I replied that this animal would be my tenth, his comment was, "You are still alive and so I trust you." I've heard of blind faith, but I had never met it before!

I finally agreed and I said that I would sit with my back to the cadaver, on the basis that the tiger would approach its kill through the long grass and would have to walk past me! Next, I fastened my torch to the fore end of the rifle and as everybody departed, we settled down to wait for the return of the maneater. We both sat through about two hours of daylight and then came the Indian twilight, leading to total darkness until the moon and the stars lit the area up. We sat there and I listened to the sounds of the jungle, in the hope that they would give me warning of the killer's return. We had been sat for about two hours, when the jungle folk stopped chattering, the tiger had returned. I sat there, straining my hearing for any sound and then I thought that I had heard something in the clump of grass. It could have been a mouse or a snake, but I didn't think it was either. Then I heard the noise, again. I couldn't let this go without investigation. It might have been nothing, in which case my actions would serve as a warning to the maneater, if he was in the vicinity. Equally, it might be something serious, like a maneater. I decided to act. I stood up and as I did so, I heard the tiger growl from about ten feet away. I thumbed the switch on the torch and illuminated the snarling face of the tiger, among the swaying stalks of grass. Before the tiger could move, I squeezed the trigger on 'Daisy' and sent an ounce and a half of nickel jacketed lead 'airmail' special. I heard the solid thud, as the bullet struck home in the chest of the maneater. In response, the maneater catapulted itself out of the grass with a loud growl and disappeared! I could hear the tiger in the undergrowth, about fifty yards away, roaring and snarling, and I told Dipak to sit tight, because I was going to have a look. I restoked 'Daisy' and started to walk over to where I could hear the tiger. As I did so, the growling increased in volume and ferocity and I realised that for whatever reason, the tiger could not run, and it was waiting for me. I was about fifteen yards from the horrific noise, when I turned the torch on to reveal the tiger, with its chest, absolutely, covered in blood and laying in a large pool of blood. It opened its jaws to roar and in doing so, it presented me with my favourite brain shot. The tiger was dead before it hit the grass, even so, I walked up and stuck the insurance round from 'May' into the back of its head. It transpired, when the tiger was examined later, that my first shot had gone into the chest, taking out the big artery over the heart and would have proved fatal in a matter of minutes. Hence the amount of blood that was being spread about by the maneater. But I am glad I did not wait and that I ended the maneater's suffering, quickly.

Why did the tiger turn to man eating? Without a doubt, the misdirected bullet from the Nawab had caused a serious wound and I suspect that the tiger thought it would be a good idea to exact retribution on the human race, for its suffering. Hence it was feeding on a mixed diet of game and humans. The wound caused by the Nawab had healed by the time I shot the maneater, but it left a very nasty scar on the tiger's flank. A classic case of a well-meaning individual not having the wherewithal to carry out his self-appointed task. I would very surprise if the Nawab ever volunteered, again. I think he learnt his lesson, the hard way. I called to see the D.M., on my way home and I told him about Dipak's help. He assured me that Dipak would be suitably recognised for his courage. Afterall, there can't be too many people who would willingly go hunting a maneater, with me!

Chapter 15

The Magadi Maneater

Magadi is a largish town, about thirty-five miles from Bangalore as the crow flies. However, the road heads north-west from Bangalore for about twenty miles and then heads south-west to reach Magadi. A total motoring distance of about fifty miles. The maneater operated around the villages of Juttanahalli, Sathanuru, and Harohalli. These were smallish villages and, so, it was not unusual for the killer to be named after the nearest town, Magadi.

The maneater was a youngish animal, being about four years old and was a tigress. The reason it took to man eating will, forever, remain shrouded in mystery. Its first victim was a wagoner on his way from Juttanahalli to Sathanuru. He had stopped by the side of the track and had climbed down from his bullock cart to answer the call of nature, when he was lifted by the tigress. The killer took her victim into the surrounding jungle and settled down to her meal. Left to their own devices, the two bullocks headed for their stable in Juttanahalli, towing the cart. When the cart arrived in the village, minus the cartman, people realised there was a problem and, initially, thought that the wagoner had met with some form of accident. A search party was organised and set off to follow the track. They eventually found a spot by the side of the track that had a few specks of rusty soil. This was blood and realising this, the search party set off to follow the spots of rust. Having travelled about two hundred yards, the group came upon what the tigress and the hyenas had left of the body and the answer was, not a lot! The body had definite evidence of death by tiger and around the body could be seen the pug marks of a youngish tigress that was slightly below average in size. Most people ascribed the death to a tragic accident and assumed that the cartman had accidently disturbed a feeding tiger or a tiger with a mate and had paid the price for his indiscretion. A tigress will often display very aggressive behaviour, when mating, and this was the mating season for tigers.

The next kill took place about a week later, when a herdsman was lifted as he was tending his herd of cattle. When the herdsman and his herd failed to return at dusk, a search party was organised the following morning and eventually the search party found the missing cattle, grazing peacefully. Signs near the area where the cattle were grazing indicated what had happened, in that there was evidence of blood and in the soft earth, the pug marks of a young tigress. The body was never found. Possibly because the search party did not look very hard, being more concerned for their own safety, and rightly so!

Within a week, there was a third kill. Another herdsman, but this time the kill was witnessed by other herdsman and the direction taken by the killer was noted. A search party was organised, and it found what was left of the cadaver, most of it had been eaten.

After the third kill, the press got hold of the story and published the usual gory and lurid accounts of what had happened, grossly embroidering the facts. I read about the actions of the tigress in the morning paper. Walking down to the local post office, I sent a telegram to the D.F.O., offering my services as a pest controller. The reply came before I had even left the post office, "Yes, please." I set off on my short journey to Magadi, where I had a talk to the D.F.O. We decided that my time would be best served if I based myself at Juttanahalli. The area was basically farmland, interspersed with pockets of trees and bushes. Ideal country for a tiger to operate in and around. I pitched my tent in a small field, just outside the village and, as usual, I had a thorn barricade set around the tent, to ensure that my slumbers were not disturbed. I spent the next few days following my usual custom of walking the area to familiarise myself with the terrain.

On the fourth day, news came of a kill near the village of Harohalli. I packed a small bag and drove down to Harohalli in my jeep. The *patel* of the village offered to show me the kill and we set off with a group of about ten men. When we got there, I found that the body had been taken into a thicket, so that the tigress could partake of her meal in peace and quiet. Very annoying, but very understandable, relatives of the deceased had arrived just before us and had taken the body away for cremation. The more I thought about the situation, the more I realised that being new to man eating, the tigress might return to her kill and start looking for the body. If she wandered about the area, looking for her kill, I might have the opportunity to shoot the killer. I decided that it would be worthwhile to sit up for the tigress and await events. My question was where? There was no tree close enough to the kill site that could help me, then I remembered a book I had read as a boy. It was called *Maneaters of Tsavo* and was written by Colonel J.H. Patterson, telling of his adventures in the 1890s, in Uganda. Colonel Patterson was faced with a similar problem to mine, a lack of suitable tree to sit in. He had constructed a tripod of about ten feet in height and had sat on a cross plank to await the return of two lions. I decided to try the same thing. I set my companions on to cut down five lengths of bamboo. Three for the tripod and two to make a ladder so that I could climb up to the seat. Whilst the men were cutting the bamboo, I was keeping a watch, just in case the tigress decided to join our work party. We used three poles of about fifteen feet in length, giving a sitting height of about twelve feet. I had the tripod backed up to a very dense bush and the ends of the poles buried in the ground, all this was to offer some protection to an attack from my rear – see *Maneater of the Babur Badans*. At about five in the evening, I climbed up to the cross piece that I was to sitting on and sat down overlooking the area where the kill had been. When the *patel* and his men had departed, the jungle settled down and I could hear a tribe of Langurs, playing, and the local birdlife was singing away.

It turned dark at about seven o'clock and I sat without moving. The moon came up and the stars came out lighting the area with a soft grey light. I had been sat for about an hour, when I noticed that the Langurs had stopped chattering and the birds of the night had fallen silent. All this told me that the tigress was near. Shortly, away to my left, I heard a twig gently creak, just once. All of these facts told me that the tigress was close, but the fact that she had trodden on a twig suggested that she was not worried or concerned about approaching her kill, or she would have made no sound, at all. I knew that the tigress was watching the area, presumably trying to locate her kill, but I heard nothing further. About an hour later, the wildlife resumed its activities and I knew that the tigress had gone. It was only about ten o'clock at night and I would have been safe in getting down from the tripod and heading back to my jeep, providing I avoided any cover likely to conceal the tigress. However, I decided to sit out the night on the off chance that the tigress might return – stubbornness being another of my many sins. As dawn broke, I had a good look around before descending the tripod. The Langurs were playing, and the birdlife was singing. I was satisfied that the tigress was not around. I climbed into my Jeep and set off for my tent at Juttanahalli, to make up for my lost sleep. I woke at about one o'clock and after a meal, drove back to Harohalli and hence, back to the thicket, to have a good look around. As I looked around, I found where the tigress had approached the thicket and where she had lain, whilst having a good look around, before moving off when she realised that her kill had gone.

The tigress made her fifth kill when she lifted a forestry worker, near to the village of Sathanuru, at about eleven o'clock in the morning. For some reason, he had become separated from his workmates and the tigress took him as he was bending down to cut some bamboo saplings. As the group heard the sounds of the man being killed, as one they took to their heels and fled! The tigress took her kill into a shallow nullah that was overgrown with grass and bushes. Three runners were sent to find me. I drove back with the three men and was told where to find the spot where the kill had taken place.

I set off to track the killer, following the blood trail and the occasional pug marks of a tigress. I had followed the killer for about half a mile, until I came to the shallow nullah that was completely overgrown, not only in the bottom, but along the top of the banks, as well. This was going to make hunting the killer very dangerous. The nullah was about three feet deep and I decided that I could hunt the killer if I could keep the wind on my back. I know what I have said about pursuing a maneater along a nullah, but there were extenuating circumstances and the nullah was only about three feet deep. It was the breeze that was the problem. The breeze was actually blowing down the nullah, towards me, and to achieve my desired goal, of making sure the killer would attack from my front, where I could deal with her, I needed the breeze to be on the back of my neck. There was only one way I could achieve this and that was by performing a big detour and entering the nullah higher up and then working my way down, towards the kill. Giving the nullah a wide berth, I walked around to a point higher up and then, I had a good look around. I could see no obvious signs of the killer in the form of pug marks or blood spatter, so I climbed down into the nullah. Again, I had a good look around, but could find no evidence that the tigress had passed this way. I checked that 'Daisy-May' was stoked-it would have been a stupid and probably fatal mistake to go chasing a maneater with an empty rifle!

Having checked my rifle, I set off down the nullah, literally, an inch at a time. I checked every bush and blade of grass, not only in the nullah, but on top of the banks as well. I was listening, also, for the sounds of feeding. I had travelled about thirty or forty yards, when I thought I could hear sounds of feeding. As I continued to edge forward, the sounds of feeding grew louder. To say that I was being careful would be a masterly understatement, yet in spite of all the care I was taking, I had overlooked the obvious! I was paying such careful attention to the sounds of the feeding tigress, that I failed to notice three magpies, sat on a branch of a tree, overlooking the kill and watching me. I calculated that I was about thirty yards from the kill when the three magpies took off squawking in alarm! The sounds of feeding ceased, abruptly, and I realised that I had a major problem and that I needed to get out of that nullah very quickly! I climbed on to the bank of the nullah, where there was a gap in the undergrowth and as I did so, a jungle cock took off about fifteen yards away in the nullah and giving its alarm call. As it did so, it flew off.

I had been right to be careful, the tigress had decided to investigate why the magpies had kicked up a fuss. I saw a slight movement in the undergrowth, not far from where the jungle cock had taken to its wings. I levelled 'Daisy-May' at the spot in the undergrowth and waited for the tigress to emerge. I stood there in absolute silence for about ten minutes, then I heard a feint noise that was coming from down the nullah. Moving very carefully, I edged my way down the nullah and eventually found the place where the tigress had deposited the body, to dine. However, the body had gone. The noise I had heard was the tigress removing the cadaver. It had taken me about twenty minutes to cover the thirty or so yards. The tigress was long gone. I could find no indication, either pug marks or blood spatter to indicate the direction taken by the killer. I spent over an hour going around in increasingly wider circles trying to find some indication of the direction in which to continue my hunt, but I found absolutely nothing! I returned to Sathanuru and my Jeep. I drove back to

Juttanahalli and after a meal and a comforting smoke of my pipe, I turned in.

The tigress made her sixth and last kill near the village of Sathanuru. A young woman of about eighteen years of age was collecting firewood with a group of women, not far from the village, when the tigress crept up under cover of some bushes and grabbed the woman, who happened to be heavily pregnant. Runners were despatched to give me the news, or *Jungli Kubbar*. I piled the runners into the back of my jeep and travelled to Sathanuru with my foot hard down on the loud pedal! On arrival at Sathanuru, I was given directions to find the place where the young woman had been killed. I set off and after a walk of about ten minutes I found where the young woman had been killed. There was a blood trail that lead through a cluster of trees that we would call a spinney, in England. The trees were fairly open, but with a few stunted bushes interspersed, as a consequence I made good progress, although I was checking every piece of cover for signs of the maneater. Once the blood trail cleared the spinney it deviated about forty-five degrees to the right and crossed an open glade that was about thirty or thirty-five yards across. The tracks led to a group of big rocks that were located on the edge of the glade. One of the biggest rocks was about fifteen feet in height and sloped backward from the vertical at an angle of about sixty degrees. Since my days in the Baden-Powell brigade (Boy Scouts) as a very young teenager, I had taken an active interest in rock climbing and this rock didn't present a challenge. Without making a sound, I climbed up and as I neared the top, I took off my hat and then slowly and carefully peered over. There was a small area of land, surrounded by rocks, the clear area being about nine feet in diameter, and I could see the young woman's body in this small space and next to the body was the tigress. Fortunately, the tigress had not started to feed, yet. The tigress was watching intently in the direction I would have travelled if I had walked around the rock, rather than performing a detour and climbing the rock. I eased 'Daisy-May' into position, being very careful to make no sound and then, for no reason I can think of or justify, I asked the question out loud.

"Are you waiting for me by any chance?"

The tigress turned her head and with a look of complete surprise on her face and got to her feet. That was as far as she was going. I squeezed the trigger and the bullet from 'Daisy' took her just behind the shoulder, taking out the heart, as I found later. The tigress dropped dead next to her victim and from on top of the rock I place a round from 'May' into the back of her head, just to make sure that she really was dead.

Getting down from the rock, I walked back towards the village to be met on the way by a large group of people who had heard my two shots. The young woman was taken back for cremation, her husband thanking me for what I had done, which in my opinion was little enough. The body of the tigress was fastened to a pole and carried back to my jeep, to be fastened on the bonnet. On my way back to Bangalore, I called to see the D.F.O. and dropped the tigress off. The tigress was skinned and apart from my two bullets, no damage could be found, or a reason given for her turning maneater. One of the mysteries of the jungle that will never be solved.

Chapter 16

Epilogue and the Mad Panther of Munchibumbum

I was, originally, supposed to spend one year living in Bangalore. In fact, I spent just short of five years living in Whitefields. John Davis, who I have mentioned earlier, had returned to the UK after one year, taking his mugger skin with him. Funnily enough, we never met again, as shortly after my return to England I joined the R.A.F. I think that there is only one reason that I was kept on in India and that reason is amply displayed in the preceding chapters. It certainly wasn't for my profound knowledge of office practice or my ability to pass on such knowledge. However, I think that my employers had decided that I had enjoyed a five-year paid holiday and that it was time for the prodigal's return. I was collected from Heathrow by my parents and even up to their deaths a few years ago, neither of them had any inkling of what I had got up to in the jungles of Southern India! They would have worried if they had known, to what effect or purpose?

Do I have any regrets about my time in India? Yes! Shooting the Manhater of Gumballi was my biggest regret. She had done nothing to deserve the treatment she received at the hands of five morons, but she could not be allowed to continue her killing spree. Do I regret shooting any of the other maneaters or rogue elephants? Most emphatically not. I have seen villagers living in abject terror because of the activities of the local wildlife. Unable and unwilling to leave the relative safety of their huts because of the fear of what might happen to them. A young boy, given the task of delivering a buffalo through a forest that was known to house a killer. A grandmother killed as she returned from visiting a new grandchild. A young woman leaving the safety of her parents' hut. No! People have the right to live free from fear and if I could contribute to the feeling of well-being by my hunting activities, then I was only too happy to oblige.

It is right and proper that I make a confession at this point. The reason I started hunting maneaters is not the reason I carried on. Originally, I simply wanted to satisfy my ego and prove to myself that I could deal with something that had ambitions on redecorating my body, as well as terminating my time on this earth! By the time I had shot my third maneater, having seen the misery they can cause, I simply wanted to help the people of southern India. This is not intended to sound arrogant or conceited, it is just a basic fact. The self-centred lad from Yorkshire had suddenly grown up! In this, I was aided and abetted by my bearer, to whom I will be eternally grateful. Thanks, Govind.

For those of you who have staved off boredom so far, let me finish with an account of the Mad Panther of Munchibumbum. I was approached by my friend Ram Gopar of the Bangalore Constabulary and told that a village about fifteen miles from Bangalore had a problem. A panther had taken up residence in a large clump of lantana and was offering to chew the living daylights out of anyone who got close enough. Ram asked me if I would just 'pop along and sort the problem'. I drove to the village and on arrival was treated to the usual signs of utter chaos, with bodies rushing in all directions and everyone shouting at the top of their voice. I was pointed in the direction of the lantana. When I reached the shrubbery, I was advised to be very careful! Me? As you all know by now, careful is my middle name! When I reached the bush, I could see pug marks leading around the lantana and I decided to follow them. When I got back to my starting point, I noticed, with more than passing interest, that the panther's pugs were, now, superimposed on mine. Whoops! Just who is following who around here? I set off again and followed the pugs around the lantana. Just as I arrived back where I had started from, I received a warning shout from several spectators.

"Behind you!" It sounded like something out of a Christmas Pantomime! I turned round to have a look and if I had been of a nervous disposition I might have died of fright. About five feet behind me and crouched ready to attack, was the panther.

Now, I haven't survived all this time by panicking and I didn't panic now. I simply turned round, bent down and picked the three-week-old cub up by the scruff of the neck! His mum had been killed by wild dogs and he and his sisters had taken refuge in the lantana. The sisters had soon been taken into care, but Laddo had decided that he was not about to give up without a fight. After I had assisted in his apprehension, he was taken to Mysore zoo and housed in a large enclosure and when he was old enough, a nice young lady panther was found, to keep him company. Just before I left India, one of the last things I did, apart from hunting the

Magadi Maneater, was to go and see my spotted playmate. I was told by zoo staff to take a chunk of meat as a gift and peace offering and throw it into his compound. Accordingly, I was taken to see 'Rajah' by one of his keepers and as he came over to the fence, I gently lobbed the piece of meat over the fencing. He picked it up and as he did so, he looked at me and I am sure that I was recognised, because he gave me the sort of look that said, 'Would you like to try and grab me by the scruff of the neck, now?' I had to concede he was safe from such indignity. He had tried to Munchimybumbum once before. There was no way he was about to get a second chance! Bye, Rajah.

We have reached the end of my misadventures, in southern India. I hope you have enjoyed the accounts of my activities in another lifetime and, hopefully, found them interesting.

Let me close with one last confession. I have always liked wildlife, but I absolutely love the big cats and this despite some of my more antisocial activities, as detailed above. If you can support Project Tiger, please do. I am sure every passing tiger will appreciate your kindness, as I will.

As I sit here, in my study, watching my youngest granddaughter making friends with a family of mice in our garden, for whom I was commanded to construct a 'Mouse House' to a very exact specification, as I close my eyes I can hear again, "*Aaaaaaar Ooooooonah*" and a voice telling me, "*Kabbadar, sher hai, sahib!*" (Look out, there's a tiger, sir!)

"*Chalo!*" (Let's go!)